Praise for STO

D0904342

"Life has become a twenty-four-hour onslaught of e-mail, text, Twitter—in both our private and work lives. There seems to be no break from the stress! Eric Parmenter's book is a welcome reminder to us all that we can, and should, step back from all of this and regain our control. It also gives useful ideas not just about what to STOP! *but what to start instead."*

Michael Gibbs
Clinical Professor of Economics
University of Chicago Booth School of Business

"Eric Parmenter has written an erudite and insightful work on the key elements that bog down so many of us. His ability to focus on these specifics gives hope to anyone who has battled the stressful time-crunch of modern life. The cogency of his presentation delights the reader. His cheerful tone warmly invites you to a better life."

Rev. Dr. Eric Albert Zimmer, MBA
Associate Professor
Mendoza College of Business
University of Notre Dame

"Eric Parmenter's unique writing style of interconnecting a historical perspective with current psychological research and personal experiences is meaningful, informative, and inspiring. STOP! *is a great work with simplistic clarity to change negative behaviors and learn how to appreciate a healthy and thriving lifestyle for self and others."*

Rose Gantner, EdD
CEO, Well Works Publishing and Consulting
Author of Workplace Wellness: Performance with a Purpose

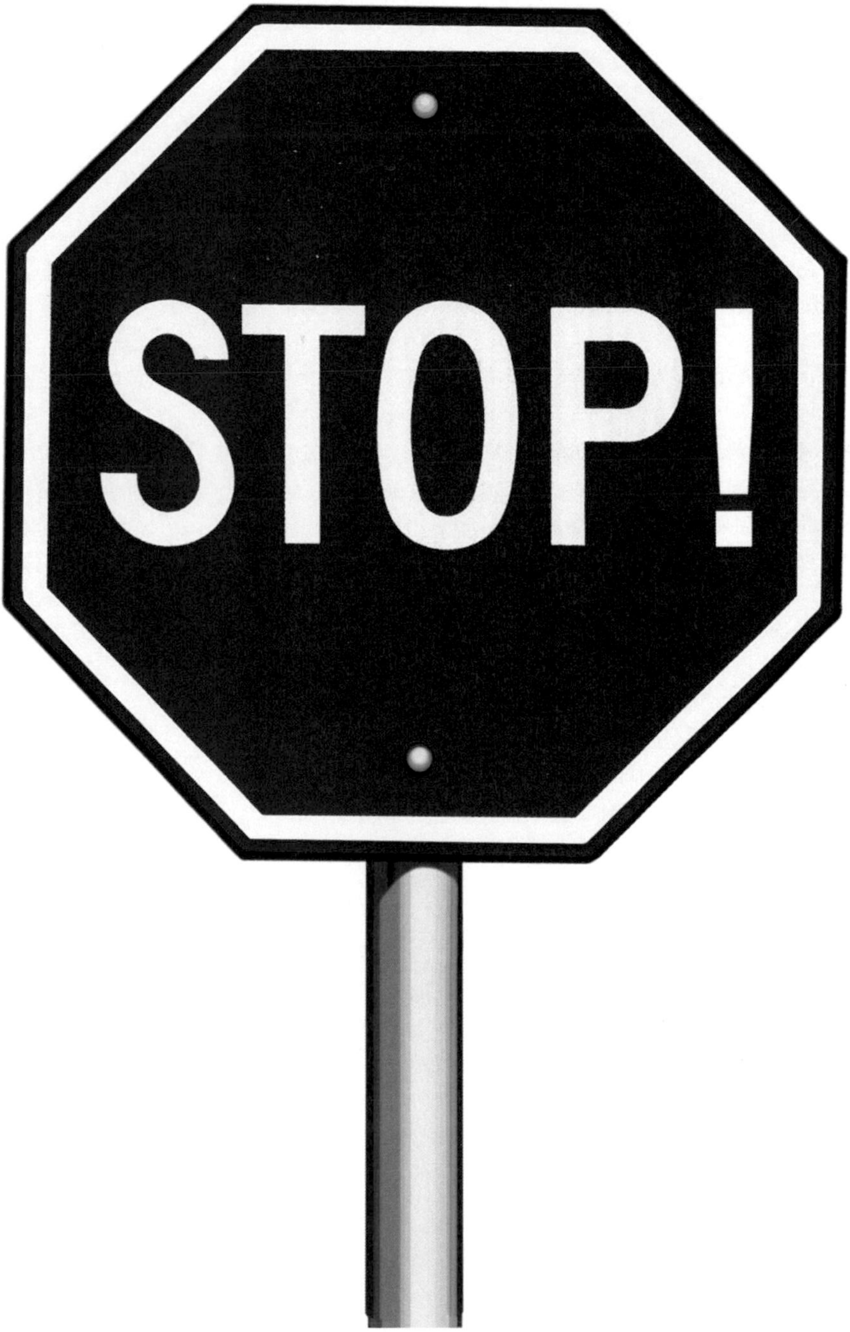
STOP!

ERIC PARMENTER

STOP!

21 STOPS TO REDUCE STRESS AND ENHANCE JOY

***BOOK*LOGIX®**
Alpharetta, GA

Scripture quotations marked (NIV) are taken from the Holy Bible, New International Version®, NIV®. Copyright © 1973, 1978, 1984 by Biblica, Inc.™ Used by permission of Zondervan. All rights reserved worldwide.

ISBN: 978-1-61005-797-4
Library of Congress Control Number: 2016909204

10 9 8 7 6 5 4 3 2   0 6 1 6 1 6

Printed in the United States of America

∞This paper meets the requirements of ANSI/NISO Z39.48-1992 (Permanence of Paper)

To our awesome kids—Natalie, Austin, Jordan, Lauren, Kelsey, Paige, and Aden—and to my best friend and wife, Sherry, who still **STOP**s *me dead in my tracks.*

Table of Contents

STOP Holding Back Your Life

Preface

The "Beginning the Journey" section of *STOP!* is essential reading to set the stage for the rest of the book. The purpose, the premise, and the point of this narrative are outlined in the introduction, so I encourage you to read it carefully before you dive in. The subsequent chapters speak to specific behaviors to **STOP**. Not all behaviors may apply to you, so feel free to read the ones that do apply and skip the ones that don't. Each chapter stands on its own. I recognize that these twenty-one behaviors are not an exhaustive list of behaviors that could be hindering your life in some way. Also, change is constant, and what holds you back today may be different from what you may struggle with at different points in your life. With changing technology and culture, behavior change is a dynamic endeavor.

However, if you discover only one practical idea that you can put to use immediately, if you can stop at least one behavior that is hindering you from experiencing more joy and less stress in your life, then I will have accomplished my goal, and you will have made a worthy investment of time and energy.

I wrote this book in the first-person voice because I wrote it initially for myself, as I need to change my life. Far too often I feel like I am wasting my time on nonessential activities or letting distractions flow into my mind, stealing my focus on my top priorities. I want to be a more focused husband, an available father, an indispensable colleague, and a trusted friend. I want to be a deep listener and a student of all the beauty and wonder in our world. I want to make a difference in the lives I touch, the health of the nation, and in myself.

Eric Parmenter
Franklin, Tennessee
May 2016

Beginning the Journey

This book is not about all the wonderful things you could do in your life. I suspect that you already know your passions and your talents. You may even have a bucket list. If not, the principles in this narrative could help you free up some time for more self-discovery. This book is about what *not* to do with your time, energy, thoughts, and resources. Fundamentally, this book is about human behavior in the inverse: it is about stopping behaviors that diminish your well-being, rob your joy, and hinder your personal performance.

STOP! is not directly about the achievement of any of the following:

- Health
- Wealth
- Greater results
- Living up to your potential
- Living your passion
- Self-actualization

My goal is to help you experience **greater joy** and **less stress** on your journey. Are you ready to add more joy and take away stress? Stress reduction and joy enhancement boost well-being and increase personal performance. Both improvements could naturally lead you to the achievements most self-help books concentrate on. My intent is centered on helping you enjoy the journey instead of being so focused on your destination that you miss the special moments along the way. *STOP!* is not a how-to book. While I do provide tips that I hope will help you take steps to **STOP** unhealthy behaviors, my goal is to shine the light on behaviors that might have a bigger impact on your life than you previously thought and to motivate you to take the next step to doing a behavior tune-up. I list several great books in the "Resources" section at the back that provides much more research, depth, and methodology on many of the topics covered in *STOP!* as well as just some of my favorite books on other topics.

In my thirty-plus years of working as a consultant and advisor to employers on health benefits and wellness programs—primarily with large hospitals and health systems—I've noticed that most of the people I encounter have stress levels that are off the charts, particularly in the wake of healthcare reform. Many healthcare workers, such as doctors and nurses, are so busy taking care of patients and trying to keep up with technology and the heavy administrative burden of medicine that they do not take care of themselves.

Far too many people run from meeting to meeting, multitasking and dealing with distractions all day long. They wind up settling into existing. They are on autopilot, locked into habits that keep them from making changes that would bring them more of what they say they want out of life. Even worse, many healthcare workers are downright burnt out, boiling with frustration, and suffering deep dissatisfaction with their careers. More than 1 million patients lose their medical doctors to suicide in this country along with a shocking number of medical students—a deeply disturbing fact that Pamela Wible, MD, tackled in her TEDMED Talk in which she addressed the high-pressure, high-stress, and sometimes abusive culture and sleep deprivation prevalent throughout the industry.[1]

By nature, I'm a pretty happy guy, but the frenetic activity I am surrounded by in the industry started to wear me down, too. And it got me thinking. Where had I allowed myself to slip into bad habits that are counterproductive to what I say I want in my life? Like the healthcare workers I serve, my own health scare with high cholesterol, weight gain, and stress made me realize that I needed to **STOP** and take a hard look at myself.

I was traveling three to four days a week and my calendar was a disaster, with back-to-back-to-back meetings and conference calls even as I trudged through an airport or flopped into the back seat of a taxicab. I joined Evolent

Health as employee No. 9 in late 2011. Working for a start-up venture is exhilarating and stressful. Our growth has been amazing and now we employ more than one thousand Evolenteers, as we call ourselves, and are traded on the New York Stock Exchange. In addition to stress at work, my wife Sherry and I got married the same year I joined Evolent and now have a blended family of seven children, five grandsons, and two more grandchildren on the way as of this writing. Figuring out our new family dynamic has been great, but also presents challenges at times. You get the picture. I needed to change myself.

There is no shortage of things on our to-do lists. The question we should be asking ourselves is not *what to do* but *what to* **STOP** *doing*. If we **STOP** and ask the right questions, we can enjoy healthier lives, be more focused and productive in our work, express our talents, do the things we enjoy, experience greater peace and richer relationships, and help others. So, perhaps you are ready to create a **STOP**-doing list.

Here are three key categories of behaviors to **STOP** immediately:

1. **STOP** ignoring your health.
2. **STOP** hindering your work.
3. **STOP** holding back your life.

If you think willpower is all it takes to **STOP** any behavior, you are dead wrong. Learning to **STOP** behavior requires you to develop new methods for making conscious, deliberate, and disciplined decisions.

We make hundreds of decisions every day. These decisions vary from the mundane to the complex, such as:

- What do I want to wear today given my schedule?
- Should I have a fruit shake for breakfast, a bowl of cereal, or just skip it because I'm late?
- Which route should I take to work based on this traffic jam?

- While playing chess with my son, what move should I make next as I predict his next set of moves?

According to Daniel Kahneman in *Thinking, Fast and Slow*,[2] the renowned psychologist and winner of the Nobel Prize in economics teaches us that we make decisions by deploying two systems—thinking fast and thinking slow. System 1 is thinking fast and is automatic, based on patterns that have developed in our brain from past experience and memory. In fast thinking, we rely on rules of thumb and preconceived notions. System 1 engages first, quickly and every time. This type of thinking comes easily because it is often unconscious. Examples of fast thinking include driving a car on an empty road. For example, have you ever arrived at your destination with no memory of the trip?

System 2 is thinking slow and is conscious, deliberate, and requires concentration, like chess moves. It is difficult, engages last, and takes more energy. Examples of slow thinking are completing a tax return or, a less taxing example, reading a menu at a restaurant and deciding what to order.

If all of our decisions required thinking slowly we would drain our energy and accomplish very little each day. These two systems are designed to work together to conserve energy and for survival.

I like to think of the two systems as two types of roads: the fast lane without stop signs and the local lanes through the town with many stops and entrances to businesses and homes as illustrated below.

Welcome to STOPVILLE

Researchers at MIT attached brain scanners to rats and placed them in mazes to find the exit. They learned that a great deal of activity took place in their cerebral cortex while learning the maze.[3] However, after numerous attempts, the rats learned the route and the cortex registered less activity.[4] The brain converts the sequence of actions into chunks or bundles and transfers those bundles down to the primitive part of the brain, the basal ganglia. This transfer frees up the cerebral cortex for good, slow thinking.[5] In this regard, we are like rats.

One way in which we think fast is to form habits. According to Charles Duhigg in *The Power of Habit*, we respond to cues, such as time of day, location, or our emotional state with routines that deliver a reward.[6] Cue, routine, and reward form the "Habit Loop."[7]

Rewards are pleasurable by definition, but habits can be good or bad. For instance, forming the routine of taking the stairs rather than the elevator not only delivers immediate pleasurable endorphins (neurotransmitters, or chemical messengers, that help relieve stress and pain) and other pleasure chemicals like dopamine, norepinephrine, and serotonin in your brain, but over time it improves your health.[8] Other habits are routines that deliver immediate pleasure, like smoking a cigarette, which delivers pleasure from increased levels of dopamine in the brain triggered by nicotine, but have harmful long-term effects.[9]

To realign our lives around healthy behavior we need to **STOP**. First, we need to get off the fast lane, pull into the pit **STOP** to do some slow thinking, and go to the lookout tower and assess our behavior objectively. Imagine you are looking down on your behavior from a tower, emotionally detached. At the next pit **STOP** we can do some more slow-thinking and begin to redesign how we make choices and swap out new routines and test different rewards that allow for new fast-thinking with pleasurable short-term and healthy long-term effects. These pit **STOPs** are like tune-ups for our brain. They allow us to **STOP** some unwanted behavior, purging the gunk of bad stress and replacing it with clean, pure-flowing well-being and joy. The key is to **STOP**.

We all deal with stressors on a daily basis. Any time we encounter something that disturbs us either mentally or physically, stress results. It's omnipresent in life. A particularly stressful event triggers the fight-or-flight response, causing hormones such as adrenaline and cortisol to surge through your body. A little bit of stress, known as "acute stress," can be exciting, and keeps us active and alert. The big problem comes in when you are dealing with long-term, chronic stress, which I call bad stress. Being under constant stress—either on the job or at home or both—can have dire detrimental effects on your health.

Ironically, studies have shown that healthcare workers and doctors are some of the most stressed-out people among all professions, and yet we are putting our health in their hands. For instance, doctors, teens, and lawyers have the worst driving records.[10] In addition, the health of our healthcare workers is worse than in just about any other industry in the United States, showing higher instances of obesity, smoking, chronic disease, and stress-related illnesses than the average employee in America.[11]

Almost anything can be a stressor, but I find this list of eleven common stress triggers listed by *Whole Living: Body+Soul in Balance* especially handy, since the ideas in *STOP!* are designed to address them:[12]

- Money issues
- A job that never ends
- A job you don't like
- Your relationships
- Constant caregiving
- Holiday pressure
- Taking on too much
- Not enough quality time
- Striving to be perfect
- Lack of passion
- Disorganized clutter

You will likely not be able to control many of the stressors in your world, but you can alter your reaction to them. This book teaches you how to quit the behaviors that leave you constantly overwhelmed and stressed. At a world health conference of leading healthcare professionals, the results of a long-term study were released that tracked whether people who'd been told that they would die in five years or less if they didn't make drastic lifestyle changes actually did so. Shockingly, only one out of every nine people elected to **STOP** doing the behaviors that had led to such a poor prognosis.

Even when faced with death, most people didn't **STOP** stressing their bodies and minds. If you're stressed out, your life may depend on how willing you are to **STOP** doing what's gotten you into your current state. Einstein said the definition of insanity was doing the same things over and over again and expecting different results.

More than 97 percent of American adults do not meet four basic characteristics of a healthy lifestyle, researchers at Oregon State University found in a study published in the Mayo Clinic Proceedings at the time of this writing. Although two-thirds had at least one or two vital healthy habits—a good diet, moderate exercise, healthy BMI, and not smoking—researchers were stunned that so few people had all four.[13] We have to **STOP** and look at ourselves.

According to the Merriam-Webster dictionary, **joy** (from the Middle English with roots from the Old French word *joie*, based on Latin *gaudium*, from *gaudere,* which means "rejoice") is the emotion evoked by well-being, success, or good fortune or by the prospect of possessing what one desires.[14]

Well-being is defined as the state of being happy, healthy, or successful. My friend Gene Harker, MD, PhD, defines well-being as a state that exists when organisms function in an environment in harmony with how they were made. A plant is in harmony with its environment when it has the proper amount of sunlight, water, and carbon dioxide and nutrients. Humans experience well-being when they are in harmony with their environment, when they know their needs and have the means to meet them while also helping to meet the needs of others.

I know when I'm in harmony with my beautiful wife Sherry—we are enjoying where we are and meeting each other's needs. I have a sense of elation from being in sync with the person I love. Did you know that as a couple, for instance, each of you gives off a sound, and when you are connected, the sounds you emit are literally in harmony with each other? Likewise, if one of you is draining the other, the sounds you emit will clash.[15]

Higher personal performance means that we perform our chosen endeavors with a greater degree of skill, talent, knowledge, or acumen. For an Olympic sprinter or swimmer, that means faster times. For a schoolteacher, high performance may mean the ability to help students master the subject matter at hand. The word **telos** (from the Greek τέλος for "end," "purpose," or "goal") means an end or purpose, used by philosophers such as Aristotle. It is the root of the term "teleology," which is roughly the study of objects with a view to their aims, purposes, or intentions.[16] Today, we define teleology as the study of personal performance.

In contrast to telos, **techne** is a term etymologically derived from the Greek word τέχνη (Ancient Greek: [tékʰnɛː]), that is translated as "craftsmanship," "craft," or "art."[17] Techne is the rational method involved in producing an object or accomplishing a goal or objective; however, the two methods are not mutually exclusive in principle.[18]

So what? Why all the definitions and Latin and Greek words? The premise of this book is that joy is not just a random emotion nor is stress out of the realm of our influence. By exercising method and purpose, you can boost your joy quotient significantly and reduce killer stress. Stopping behaviors that hold you back from your chosen, purposeful pursuits requires the practice of new methods based on new rules. Restructuring your life to "not go there" and nixing unwanted behaviors is an art form, a craft, a method. The method that I've adopted and I'm asking you to use enables you to intentionally **STOP** the behaviors that crowd our minds, that take our time, that drain our energy and distract us from the pursuit of our purpose and passion.

With these barriers removed and energy sappers zapped, we can focus on our strengths, talents, and experiences that bring joy and reduce stress for the people in our lives and for us. This method gives us the ability to **STOP** the madness—the barrage of stimuli in our technologically frenzied society combined with our own unhealthy habits that lead to misery, the antonym of joy.

The problem is too much noise and too much stuff. I am inundated by clutter everywhere, especially in my mind. We live in a world where, if we lack the ability to discipline our minds, our minds quickly fill up with noise and distractions.

We need less, not more.

Do you feel like you have more time and energy or less? Do you have as much time and energy as you would like to think, reflect, meditate, plan, read, write, paint, enjoy your hobby or avocation, exercise, and engage with the most important people in your life? If the answer to any of these questions is *no*, it is time to **STOP**.

Jim Collins, author of the business classic *Good to Great*, talks about the 20-10 assignment: "Suppose you woke up tomorrow and received two phone calls. The first phone call tells you that you have inherited $20 million, no strings attached. The second tells you that you have an incurable and terminal disease, and you have no more than [ten] years to live. What would you do differently, and, in particular, what would you stop doing?"[19] Collins goes on to describe how that assignment became a turning point in his life. Asking himself those two questions caused a shift in how he allocates his most precious resource: time. I encourage you to think about this 20-10 exercise as you read this book. Life is short, time is precious, and I have never heard of anyone making this deathbed proclamation: "I wish I would have spent more time at the office completing my to-do list."

Not all twenty-one **STOP**s will apply to you. There may be many other behaviors that you need to **STOP** in your life that are not covered in these pages. These behaviors are taken from my life experience and yours may be different. Whether you **STOP** just a few of the twenty-one behaviors or most of them, my hope is that you will tap into new potential in your life.

Each one of us is uniquely gifted. I desire to live more in my giftedness and less in areas that do not require my uniqueness. If you want the same in your life, decide what you can **STOP** doing long enough to read this book. May it bring joy to your life and the lives of those you touch, and we all touch so many other lives.

My favorite movie of all time is Frank Capra's *It's a Wonderful Life*, starring the legendary Jimmy Stewart and Donna Reed. The awkward angel Clarence spoke a great truth when he said, "Strange, isn't it? Each man's life touches so many other lives. When he isn't around he leaves an awful hole, doesn't he?"

My wish for you is that you will **STOP** any behavior that will prevent you from living a long, healthy, and wonderful life.

CHAPTER 1

STOP Eating Too Much

I had a missed call. It's probably the all-you-can-eat buffet calling to say, "Come back! We know you can eat just a little bit more."

— Jarod Kintz

This book is not a diet book. Far be it from me to add to the thousands of books written on diet and nutrition. Most of us know that we should eat fewer artery-clogging trans fats, sugar, and processed foods and eat more fresh fruits and vegetables. When it comes to eating, my message is simple:

- **STOP** eating too much by reducing portion size.
- **STOP** eating three big meals a day. Instead, eat several small meals or snacks throughout the day to regulate energy.
- **STOP** eating foods that drain energy, like sugar and empty carbs. Eat a combination of healthy foods that give you energy and foods you really enjoy.

Many of us grew up with parents who taught us to "clean your plate." My grandparents, the late Leonard and Virginia Key, survived the Great Depression of the early 1930s and were keen to not waste anything of value, especially scarce food. My grandparents embraced Benjamin Franklin's admonition: "Waste not, want not."

When that thought has been drilled into your head, pushing back from the table before your plate is empty may produce a twinge of guilt.

Compounding the problem is that dinner plates in homes and restaurants have almost doubled in size along with portions. No wonder belonging to the "clean-plate club" now means that you're probably overeating.

Portions and Calories 20 Years Ago Compared to Present Day

| | 20 Years Ago | | Today | |
	Portion	Calories	Portion	Calories
Bagel	3" diam.	140	6" diam.	350
Cheeseburger	1	333	1	590
Spaghetti w/ Meatballs	1 cup sauce 3 small meatballs	500	2 cups sauce 3 large meatballs	1020
Soda	6.5 oz	82	20 oz	
Blueberry Muffin	1.5 oz	210	5 oz	

Do you often feel drowsy after a large meal and feel your energy sag? Do you seek comfort in food or eat more than you should because you are enjoying the taste? When you eat too much, you exact a toll on your body. Overeating stresses your system because it requires redirecting extra energy to the process of digestion. An overloaded system simply stores those extra calories as fat when the excess can't be eliminated properly.

I like Harvard Medical School's recommendations on healthy eating, particularly as they relate to energy. According to Harvard, a balanced diet includes a variety of unrefined carbohydrates, proteins, and beneficial fats, with an emphasis on vegetables, whole grains, and healthy oils. Taking a daily multivitamin helps you get the vitamins and minerals you need, but taking extra amounts of individual nutrients won't give you more energy.

Eat certain types of foods in the right amounts to prevent fatigue. Different kinds of foods are converted to energy at different rates. Candy gives you a quick lift, but then the sugar rush causes your energy levels to crash. Whole grains and complex carbohydrates balanced with protein like raw nuts provide energy reserves throughout the day. Occasional treats are okay if you must indulge, but limit refined sugar as much as possible. Sugar's quick boost fades fast and leaves you craving another dose.

Eat for energy. STOP consuming three large meals a day. For better energy and brain function, you need to eat small meals and snacks every few hours. This approach reduces your perception of fatigue because your brain, which has few energy reserves of its own, needs a steady supply of nutrients. Some people begin feeling sluggish after just a few hours without food. But it doesn't take much to feed your brain. A small piece of fruit like an apple with a tablespoon of almond butter or a handful of nuts suffices.

The circadian rhythms of people who eat a lot at lunch typically show a more pronounced afternoon slump, research shows. This slump likely reflects the increase in blood sugar after eating, which is followed by a dip in energy.[20]

I love to eat. I am particularly smitten with all the bad stuff: steaks (I prefer a rib-eye medium rare) and loaded baked potatoes (butter, sour cream, cheddar cheese, bacon bits, and chives, thank you very much). I rarely pass up a piece of key lime pie, and my wife, Sherry, makes an amazing red velvet cake, not to mention her famous coconut cake. I could go on and on, but I'm beginning to drool. But with high cholesterol and weight gain, not to mention sluggishness, I have changed some of my eating patterns.

Sherry is a good influence on me, since she has maintained her high school weight through exercise and watching what she eats. At times since our marriage, I've struggled, especially since I love food so much. Since we're both in our fifties, our metabolism has slowed down. We've learned that the key for us is eating healthily most of the time, limiting portion sizes, and allowing ourselves an occasional indulgence. Dessert should be a treat—not a regular part of your meal, like it was when we grew up.

Normally, when Sherry and I are home, we enjoy a power shake in the morning with fresh fruit, yogurt, and natural protein powder. By midmorning our energy levels dip, and we have a small snack: an apple with reduced-fat peanut butter is a favorite. A salad or turkey sandwich on whole-wheat bread makes a great lunch followed by a fifteen- to thirty-minute nap. By the way, when did Americans stop taking naps? My grandparents took a nap after lunch every day, and they accomplished more on their farm daily than most non-nappers. Naps are a lost art and indulgent pleasure, not to mention a ritual that provides health benefits.

By midafternoon our energy dips again, and I might have some almonds or pecans. A healthy dinner with fish or chicken and veggies, or just veggies, hits the spot with a small snack before bedtime to round out the day.

I know that I would be better off not eating red meat. However, I enjoy a good steak once in a while. We live in Nashville, Tennessee, which features some of the best meat and some of the best hot chicken you've ever tasted—none of which rate as healthy choices. In my opinion, occasionally indulging in your favorite foods, even if they do not qualify as the healthiest, is perfectly okay, so long as it's done in moderation. The vegetarian or vegan lifestyle can be healthy, and I applaud those who adhere to it, but it's not my cup of tea. By the way, a spot of tea is a great, relaxing, healthy drink, and green and white teas are packed with antioxidants. Green tea even boosts your metabolism.

We often travel for my work and love to vacation in new places. One of our favorite avocations is eating out at popular local restaurants. We are foodies, but Sherry and I often share an entrée, not only to save money but also to help with portion control. We prefer menu items where the ingredients are sourced from local farms and organic. We always ask if fish is wild-caught, too, because farmed fish has much less nutritional value. For example, recent studies show that tilapia, which is almost exclusively farmed, is often fed soy-based feed, which many people are supposed to limit in their diets due to soy raising estrogen toxicity in their systems.[21]

I am a gadget guy. I use a digital scale and blood-pressure monitor that syncs with activity, and a sleep tracker, which in turn syncs with my nutrition tracker, all through smartphone apps. These apps provide great data and coaching tips. They also keep you honest and give you detailed information that you can share with your doctor if you choose. I enter my food intake into my nutrition-tracker app, which can be annoying at times, but it only takes a few seconds and allows me to know empirically what I know intuitively: whether I am eating too much. Do I always **STOP** eating too much? No. But at least I have a plan, and these gadgets help me manage weight and, more importantly, experience the joy that comes from delicious food and higher energy.

A key discipline of eating for energy and portion control is eating mindfully. In our grab-and-go, fast-food society, too often we stuff food in our mouth, quickly chew, and swallow without thinking. We often eat mindlessly to pass time, grazing during sporting events, eating at our desk at work. Brian Wansink, PhD, has written a wonderful book called *Mindless Eating,* and he writes that "studies show that the average person makes around 250 decisions about food every day," adding that "after conducting hundreds of studies, I'm increasingly convinced that our stomach has only three settings: 1) We either feel like we're starving, 2) we feel like we're stuffed, or 3) we feel like we can eat more. Most of the time we're in the middle, we're neither hungry nor full, but if something is put in front of us, we'll eat it."[22]

Do you gobble your food? I certainly do—more than I would like to admit. Develop the discipline to take smaller bites, savor the flavors in your mouth, chew a few more times, and take a break before the next bite. Slowing down and enjoying your food has many benefits. One of those benefits can be existential, as wonderfully described by Kahlil Gibran, author of the classic book *The Prophet*:

"And when you crush an apple with your teeth, say to it in your heart: Your seeds shall live in my body, And the buds of your tomorrow shall blossom in my heart, And your fragrance shall be my breath, And together we shall rejoice through all the seasons."

—*Kahlil Gibran*

Another benefit of slower, more mindful eating is that it helps with portion control. The faster you eat, generally the more you eat. By eating slowly, you can make the dining experience last as long as the conversation with your dining companions. Your digestion improves when you eat more slowly, too. Food that is thoroughly chewed goes down easier with less risk of choking. Finally, eating mindfully allows us to take time to use our senses to take in our food's appearance, the nuances of flavor, the different spices, textures, and smells.

Mindful eating goes beyond the actual consumption of food. It includes the selection and preparation of food. When shopping in a grocery store, **STOP** browsing the aisles in the middle of the store. That's where the processed foods in boxes, cans, jars, and bags tend to be stocked. Instead, make a habit of concentrating solely on the perimeter of the store where you'll find fresh produce and natural and organic foods.

An even better bet: spend some time on the weekend at your local farmers' market where you can get fresh, local foods in season. You'll be supporting small local businesses and helping the environment while helping yourself to better health. ***Tip:*** Get there early, because savvy regulars know who has the best offerings and farmers' produce can sell out fast.

When you prepare meals at home, you know exactly what ingredients are in the food. You can avoid chemical-laden processed foods and produce doused in pesticides. You are in control. Preparing food can be entertaining and relaxing at the same time. Sherry and I love working in the kitchen together while talking with friends and loved ones and sipping a glass of wine. Taking part in every step of the process provides a fun way to bond and sparks great conversation. Once the meal is served, a feeling of accomplishment accompanies the dining experience because you had a hand in making it happen.

Eating **mindfully**, eating **smaller meals and snacks** throughout the day, and eating **healthy, natural foods for energy** have all been scientifically proven to lower bad stress and enhance our joy by boosting energy. When you **STOP** eating too much, you gain a happier, healthier you.

Questions for Reflection

- Do you eat three meals a day or several small ones?
- Do you use small plates when serving meals at home?
- Do you split meals with your spouse or a friend?

CHAPTER 2

STOP Drinking Too Much

In all things moderation, including moderation.

—Arnold Beckman

To me, enjoying a glass of wine with friends and family at dinner or a cocktail with my wife and friends after work presents a wonderful way to unwind and enhance conversation and connectedness. For this lifelong, avid St. Louis Cardinals fan, drinking a cold beer on a hot afternoon at the baseball park ranks high on my list of life's pleasures. However, some of us need a little reminder that the consumption of alcohol in excess often leads to devastating consequences, whether immediate—such as physical altercations, automobile accidents, and suicide—or long-term addiction and damage to our bodies.

If you do not drink, good for you. Abstinence is obviously the safest route. If you drink, know when to **STOP**. Develop some rules of thumb that set appropriate limits. Here are some boundaries that could help:

- I will limit myself to two drinks a day (for men). I will limit myself to one drink a day (for women).
- I will limit myself to three days of drinking in a week.
- I will ask someone to remind me of my limits if I have difficulty sticking to them.
- If I can't stick to my limits, I need some help and won't be embarrassed or ashamed to ask.

Dr. Gene Harker tells a story in his book *Pause Points* about children playing on a school playground surrounded by a chain-link fence. The school officials removed the fence because they did not want the schoolyard to look like a prison. The children, who used to play all over the grounds, right up to the fence, now stayed close to the building and avoided the area where the fence once stood. The fence provided the children with a sense of security and safety and allowed them more freedom.[23] Having boundaries about alcohol consumption does the same for adults, and we all need the security and safety of boundaries if we drink alcohol.

There have been times when I was drinking too much. I have gone cold turkey at times and set limits at other times. By setting strong boundaries for yourself, you greatly diminish the danger that you'll make a poor decision while under the influence that could have devastating lifelong consequences for you or others. When you have poorly defined boundaries, you compromise who you are. The loss of freedom and control that accompanies intoxication is frightening. There is no shortage of news accounts where celebrities and ordinary folks do foolish things they later regret, and that's if they come out on the other side alive.

According to the National Institute on Alcohol Abuse and Alcoholism, the toll from alcohol use disorders is heavy, to say nothing of the economic burden, which is estimated at more than $200 billion per year, mostly from binge drinking.[24]

Alcohol Use Disorders (AUDs) in the United States

1. **Adults (ages 18+):** 16.3 million adults ages 18 and older (6.8 percent of this age group) had an AUD in 2014. This includes 10.6 million men (9.2 percent of men in this age group) and 5.7 million women (4.6 percent of women in this age group).
   - About 1.5 million adults received treatment for an AUD at a specialized facility in 2014 (8.9 percent of adults who needed

treatment). This included 1.1 million men (9.8 percent of men in need) and 431,000 women (7.4 percent of women who needed treatment).

2. **Youth (ages 12–17):** In 2014 an estimated 679,000 adolescents ages 12–17 (2.7 percent of this age group) had an AUD. This number includes 367,000 females (3.0 percent of females in this age group) and 311,000 males (2.5 percent of males in this age group).

•   An estimated 55,000 adolescents (18,000 males and 37,000 females) received treatment for an alcohol problem in a specialized facility in 2014.

3. **Alcohol-Related Deaths:** Nearly 88,000 people (approximately 62,000 men and 26,000 women) die from alcohol-related causes annually, making it the third leading preventable cause of death in the United States.

•   In 2014, alcohol-impaired driving fatalities accounted for 9,967 deaths (31 percent of overall driving fatalities).[25]

These facts related to alcohol use in the United States are alarming and are a sobering (pun intended) reminder of why alcohol abuse was recently named by the World Health Organization as the No. 1 health problem in the world. A person dies from alcohol-related problems every six seconds, yet alcohol consumption is so prevalent in our society that we accept these problems as normal, notes Al J. Mooney, MD, coauthor of *The Recovery Book* and director of Addiction Medicine and Recovery at Willingway Hospital in Statesboro, Georgia. "We glamorize drinking, yet it's so destructive. Almost 10 [percent] of the country's population suffers from addiction in some form to alcohol or drugs."[26]

Part of the problem is that—just like with food—alcohol is much more readily available now. We can buy it at the grocery store, and it's invariably a key component of virtually every social event. Research shows that most people don't understand what constitutes one drink, nor do they understand that the amount of alcohol in a single drink varies widely. Our perception often depends on the size of the glass in which the drink is served. Because we don't realize how much we're drinking, we quickly negate any of the industry's much-touted health benefits of drinking wine.

Many recently released studies and recommendations emphasize that alcohol consumption should be curtailed more strictly than previously thought—especially for women. The Centers for Disease Control (CDC) came out in February 2016 officially recommending that women of childbearing age avoid alcohol consumption entirely.[27]

So what should you do? The official CDC recommendations are no more than one drink a day for women and two drinks a day for men. Most experts in the field are even more conservative, especially for women: If you do drink, limit yourself to one glass of wine—no more than 5 ounces—or one serving of an alcoholic drink every few days, so that your liver can recover.

In the United States, a standard drink contains 0.6 ounces (14.0 grams or 1.2 tablespoons) of pure alcohol. According to the CDC, generally, this amount of pure alcohol is found in:

- 12 ounces of beer (5 percent alcohol content).
- 8 ounces of malt liquor (7 percent alcohol content).
- 5 ounces of wine (12 percent alcohol content).
- 1.5 ounces of 80-proof (40 percent alcohol content) distilled spirits or liquor (e.g., gin, rum, vodka, whiskey).

Keep in mind that hard liquor, which is made from rice, agave, or potatoes, contains high levels of sugar, which is bad for you. Fruity drinks compound the problem. One frozen margarita contains one hundred grams of sugar versus Ben & Jerry's ice cream, which has twenty-five grams of sugar per cup—two cups in a pint. The cold beer I like to drink at a baseball game is similar to eating bread. In most cases, wine is your best choice if you decide to drink.

As we age, we don't metabolize alcohol as quickly and efficiently as we used to, which leads to weight gain. Compounding the problem—a large percentage of the population is on prescription drugs, or takes over-the-counter (OTC) medications like aspirin, or supplements. The combination of alcohol and any or all of these can quickly turn your liver toxic or even become deadly. Don't assume that because your doctor prescribed something, it's safe to mix with your nightly cocktail, or that it's safe to have a couple glasses of wine with the OTC meds you take for your aches and pain. Talk to your pharmacist or doctor about what you are taking and your level of consumption. The CDC calls accidental overdose from mixing alcohol and drugs an epidemic.

So why is alcohol so damaging? It damages every organ in your body, especially the liver, which is already dealing with genetically modified organisms (GMOs), pesticides, and other toxins. Give your liver a break. It needs a chance to detoxify. The liver has a hard time processing alcohol, and many people are missing an enzyme necessary to process it at all. Because alcohol is a diuretic, drinking drains your body of B vitamins and magnesium. The risk of cancer goes up dramatically for drinkers. Over-consumption also leads to thyroid problems, which puts a strain on your sex hormones. Long-term alcohol abuse changes your brain's function, causing poor decision making.

As you consider your level of consumption, here are some factors to keep in mind:

- How much you drink
- What you drink
- How often you drink
- Your age
- Your sex

- Your family history
- Your health

Arnold O. Beckman, the son of a blacksmith, grew up to play a pivotal role in the instrumentation revolution that dramatically changed science, technology, and society. From his rural boyhood world of farming and woodworking, through his service in the US Marines and his appointment to the CalTech faculty, to his path-breaking creation of the pH meter, the DU spectrophotometer, and the establishment of the Beckman Instruments Company, he achieved great success.[28] In 1984, my alma mater, the University of Illinois (U of I), was the beneficiary of a generous $40 million gift from Beckman, which led to the founding of the Beckman Institute for Advanced Science and Technology.[29]

By winning a door prize, I got a wonderful opportunity to tour the Beckman Institute and to have lunch with the Nobel-Prize-winning physicist (2003) along with Anthony Leggett, who works at the Beckman Institute. I invited my dear friend LaMarr Barnes to join me. I'm so glad that LaMarr accompanied me on this tour and lunch because I know virtually nothing about physics, and LaMarr has a degree in physics from the U of I. On the tour, we witnessed 3-D printers in action and saw some of the most sophisticated research laboratories in the world. However, the item that struck me the most during this visit was a placard that hung on the wall of the entrance:

Arnold O. Beckman's
RULES for SUCCESS

* There is no satisfactory substitute
for excellence

*Absolute integrity . . . in everything

*Everything in moderation . . .
including moderation itself

*Hire the best people
and then get out of
their way

These simple rules are profound. With respect to alcohol, if we strive for excellence and integrity in all that we do, we must accept appropriate boundaries. There are times when a little less moderation is okay as long as you practice safety and have boundaries. That cartoon philosopher

Homer Simpson said, "Alcohol is a way of life, and it's my way of life, and I aim to keep it." Well, alcohol is a way of life for many people today. However, as with most things in life, too much of a good thing can be dangerous.

The solution is simple but not easy. **STOP** drinking too much. For those for whom alcohol is an addiction and cannot stop taking a drink, total abstinence has been proven to be the only viable solution. Alcoholics Anonymous is based on this principle—staying sober one day at a time. For the rest of us, follow Beckman's *Rules for Success*.

Questions for Reflection

- Do you know someone who has experienced tragedy related to drinking?
- Has anyone expressed concern about your drinking?
- Do you have rules of thumb for drinking, such as no more than three days per week?

CHAPTER 3

STOP Sitting Too Much

*If we could give every individual the right amount of nourishment and exercise,
not too little and not too much, we would have found the safest way to health.*
—Hippocrates

Although we all know that working some type of physical activity into
our schedules is important every day, most of us fail to make it a priority.
Over the last several decades, our society has grown more and more
sedentary—especially as our reliance on computers, electronics, and
smartphones has increased. We joke about being couch potatoes and
living online. Yet, when I travel outside the United States, I notice how
much walking and biking are naturally a part of people's lives, and I rarely
see anyone overweight. We've got to **STOP** sitting too much.

Consider how much the average person sits in a day from driving
during a morning commute to an eight-hour-a-day desk job and then
driving home to unwind on the couch in front of the television all
evening. With today's technology, we walk less for routine tasks because
we depend on e-mail, smartphone apps, direct-deposit paychecks, and

---

*"If you take a brisk, fifteen-minute walk in the afternoon, you'll be
far more productive in your last two hours."*

— Fabio Comana

online shopping to accomplish tasks that ten or twenty years ago would have required us to get up and run errands.

As a child I was extremely active. My brother Todd and I played outside all day long from a pickup game of baseball in the backyard with the kids in the neighborhood to climbing trees. By the time I graduated from high school, I had played organized sports including basketball, football, wrestling, and track. I was never a great athlete and rarely played on the first-team varsity squad, except for wrestling, but I was very athletic. I lifted weights and would run five miles per day in high school just to train. I continued my active lifestyle throughout college, playing basketball with friends daily after class.

Once I entered the full-time working world, I let my activity slip and spent far too much time in the car, often relying on fast food for lunch and winding up too tired at the end of the long day to work out. I have been off and on ever since, but have become a little more disciplined about exercise in the past five years. It helps that Sherry is active and sets a good example. In fact, recent research shows that your partner's level of fitness and weight can influence yours, and, likewise, the company you keep matters, too. If your friends tend to be sedentary and overweight, you are far more likely to be overweight as well.

I try to reach ten thousand steps on my fitness tracker daily and log at least three to five additional workouts per week. I often run in the neighborhood or work out at the fitness center. I pack my running shoes and shorts so I can work out when I travel at the hotel fitness center, or if the weather is nice, take a walk or run outside. I also keep a balance between weight lifting and aerobic exercise. For me, exercise is not only about weight management and heart health, but also about keeping energy high and my mind clear. I find exercise gives the best opportunity to stop attending to other things, so that I can listen to TED Talks and other programs of interest on my smartphone.

For instance, I recently completed the Ken Burns documentary *Baseball* and biographies of Thomas Jefferson, Mark Twain, Ronald Reagan, and

John F. Kennedy, all while exercising. Scientific research shows that walking stimulates the areas of your brain that help you come up with creative ideas and solutions to challenges. That's why epiphanies often strike us when we are doing something physical. Ideally, start moving with a morning workout. The boost in your metabolism lasts for several hours after you work out.

Getting out in nature yields big health bonuses. A brisk hike in the woods exposes you to negative ions put off by trees, which your body craves, and increases your oxygen levels. Just a few hours spent in nature over a weekend provide a significant boost in endorphins and the immune system, lowers blood pressure, reduces inflammation and stress levels, and improves your mood. For more than three decades, *Shinrin-yoku*, which translates to "forest bathing"—the practice of spending dedicated and mindful time among trees—has been popular in Japan and Korea, and the practice is now becoming popular in the United States.

Research by Qing Li, MD, a professor at Nippon Medical School in Tokyo who studies forest medicine, shows that the positive effects of a three-day, two-night stay in the woods last up to thirty days.[30] He attributes the increase in natural killer cell activity, our bodies' immune protection, to breathing in wood essential oils, antimicrobial volatile organic compounds emitted from trees. Being near a body of water like the ocean gives off negative ions, too, which explains why we feel so much better after playing at the beach or exploring the woods. Maybe that's why we love the beach!

For instance, when we travel we like to get out and explore. Spending time outside is a double bonus: new experiences stimulate our brains, and we get to know a new area. Working out in nature also gives us a better workout, because, by navigating different terrain, we're using our balance and working out our functional muscles more.

If you are limited to working out on a treadmill, looking at scenes of nature offers some benefit too, according to research. Look for ways to change up your workout so that your muscle memory is challenged.

A growing body of research shows that long periods of physical inactivity raise your risk of developing heart disease, diabetes, cancer, and obesity. In

January 2010, British experts linked prolonged periods of sitting to a greater likelihood of disease. Australian researchers reported that each hour spent watching TV is linked to an 18 percent increase in the risk of dying from cardiovascular disease—perhaps because that time is spent sitting down.[31]

All we need to do is look around to realize that obesity is a major problem in the United States. The rate of obesity has increased steadily from around 10 percent of the American population in 1960 to more than 35 percent in 2015.[32] If this trend continues, shockingly half of Americans will be obese by 2030.

Half of the US Population Obese by 2030[33]

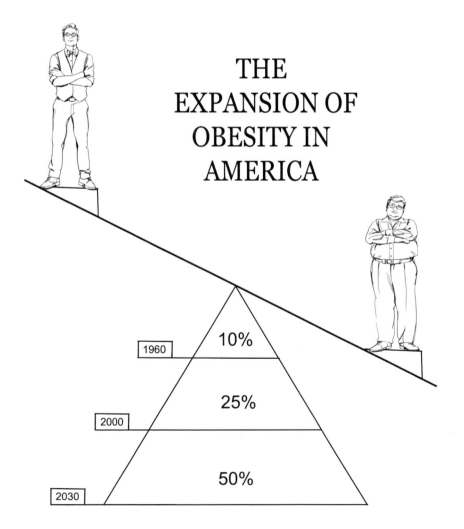

THE EXPANSION OF OBESITY IN AMERICA

1960 — 10%
2000 — 25%
2030 — 50%

In addition to proper nutrition and not overeating, the best way to avoid or reduce obesity is through routine exercise. The American College of Sports Medicine recommends that, ideally, you engage in moderate-intensity cardiorespiratory exercise training—brisk walking, for example—for 30 minutes or more five or more days per week for a total of at least 150 minutes per week. In addition, you should be getting vigorous-intensity cardiorespiratory exercise training—Zumba, kickboxing, or the like—for at least 20 minutes or more for three or more days per week for a total of 60 minutes per week.

To improve muscle tone, you need to perform resistance exercises—like weight training, during which you can use your own body weight—for each of the major muscle groups. You also need neuromotor exercise—yoga, tai chi, or the like—involving balance, agility, and coordination. Crucial to maintaining joint range of movement, you should complete a series of flexibility exercises—again, yoga works—for each of the major muscle-tendon groups two or more days a week. I bet if you add all these up, you'll realize that you aren't investing nearly enough time in your physical self. Your exercise program should be modified according to your habitual physical activity, physical function, health status, exercise responses, and your stated goals.[34]

My employer, Evolent Health, takes well-being seriously. It has installed a number of walking desks and regularly promotes the Corporate Performance Athlete initiative that was started by our CEO Frank Williams, who leads by example. He challenges all of the executives at Evolent to think like Corporate Performance Athletes. This initiative is not just another wellness program, but an effort to promote training and preparation for sustained energy in the high-stress industry of healthcare. This initiative is based on individuals achieving peak performance by training for increased energy through the High Performance Pyramid.

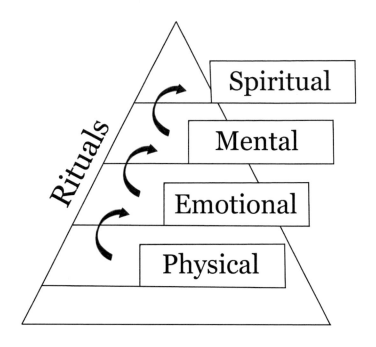

The illustration is adapted from the work of Jim Loehr and Tony Schwartz, "The Making of a Corporate Athlete," published in the *Harvard Business Review*[35] and their book *The Power of Full Engagement: Managing Energy, Not Time, Is the Key to High Performance and Personal Renewal.*[36]

The foundation of the pyramid is physical capacity and developing rituals that build endurance and promote mental and emotional recovery from the stress of our busy lives. Emotional, mental, and spiritual capacity are added to this foundation. The key to tapping into energy that leads to peak performance is in rituals, which requires a deliberate effort to **STOP** allowing our calendars to become jam-packed with calls, meetings, and energy-draining activities.

A big part of this approach is executed via scheduling rituals in our calendars. As a result, I put my workouts, walking breaks, and preparation time on my calendar. I color-code all of my commitments so others who have access to my calendar know that I am protecting high-priority preparation slots and my workouts as much as important meetings.

What does this discussion about calendars have to do with the corporate athlete and physical energy? Everything! These rituals allow me to **STOP** sitting, to build in workouts and walking breaks, and to have walking meetings with colleagues rather than booking a conference room. Like any athlete training for a sport, the solution resides in scheduled training and stopping the behaviors that drain your energy. The solution is simple, but not easy: **STOP** eating too much, drinking too much, and sitting too much. Get moving to reduce stress and find more joy.

Questions for Reflection

- How many hours do you sit on an average day?
- Do you ever have walking meetings or walk while you take phone calls?
- Do you schedule breaks on your calendar to get up and move?

CHAPTER 4

STOP Being Unconscious

Control of consciousness determines the quality of life.
—*Mihaly Csikszentmihalyi,*
Flow: The Psychology
of Optimal Experience

Close your eyes . . .

Breathe deeply . . .

Focus on your body as you breathe . . .

Think about a calm, relaxing ocean wave coming over your body
as you breathe in . . .

Think about the wave receding down your body as you breathe
out . . .

Repeat . . .

Does this sound familiar? Does it remind you of a meditation class? Mindfulness has recently become the buzzword from experts in both mental and physical health. Mindfulness is paying attention to the present moment with intention, while letting go of judgment, as if our life depends on it, says expert Jon Kabat-Zinn, PhD, founding executive director of the Center for Mindfulness in Medicine, Health Care, and Society at the University of Massachusetts Medical School.[37] And as it turns out, your life does depend on learning to be more in the moment. The time has come to **STOP** being unconscious and simply drifting through life on autopilot.

Kabat-Zinn, founding director of University of Massachusetts Medical School's renowned Stress Reduction Clinic, says that the present is the only real moment we have. But what I've noticed in my own life and those of many people is the tendency to allow our energy to be fragmented by either ruminating about the past or worrying about the future. Dwelling on past mistakes or fretting about what might happen tomorrow steals your joy and lowers the energy vibration that each of us emits.

Did you know that you can literally change your brain for the better by using mindful meditation? Surprisingly, neuroscience has proven it. The old wisdom taught that your brainpower starts to decline in middle age. The good news is that your brain is the most changeable part of your whole body and can form new neurons and new connections well into an advanced age.

"Our brain peaks at age forty-eight mainly because we let our brains decline—not because it has to," says Sandra Chapman, PhD, a cognitive neuroscientist, founder and chief director of the Center for Brain Health at The University of Texas at Dallas, and author of *Make Your Brain Smarter*.[38] "A lot of people think they don't have to worry about brain health until they are older, but what you do in your thirties, forties, and fifties and beyond matters. Your brain changes moment to moment."

The work of Richard Davidson, PhD, a cognitive scientist at the University of Wisconsin-Madison, proved that Buddhist monks meditating on unconditional loving kindness—compassion meditation—produced thirty times more gamma waves than the nonmeditating control group.[39] Plus, the monks' brains lit up in much larger areas during meditation, especially in the left prefrontal cortex, which is where positive emotions reside.[40]

In 2008, positive psychologist Barbara Fredrickson, PhD, revealed results of a study of 139 working adults—half of whom were trained in compassion meditation—showing that those who practiced meditation daily achieved big gains in joy thanks to feeling more purpose in their lives, more social support, and decreased illness symptoms.[41] In another study, an eight-week Mindfulness-Based Stress Reduction (MBSR) course given to 174 adults demonstrated that mindfulness improved significantly in all subjects, and along with that came a significant boost in joy and lower stress, both of which are my goals in this book.[42] Fascinatingly, the part of the brain where empathy resides gained volume in the subjects who participated in the study, demonstrating that, just as weight training improves muscle mass, you can literally change your brain by what you focus on.[43]

Among its many benefits, mindfulness meditation has actually been proven to increase telomerase, the "caps" at the end of our genes, which, in turn, can reduce cell damage and lengthen our lives. In addition, research demonstrates that mindfulness bolsters our immune system, making us better able to fight off diseases, from a cold to cancer. Mindfulness helps improve our concentration and reduce ruminative thinking that contributes to the high levels of stress so prevalent in our society. Stress and ruminative thinking—being stuck on a negative experience—are not only mental health hazards, but they are, quite often, the symptoms that lead people to seek the help of a therapist.

Mindfulness is an incredible tool to help us understand, tolerate, and deal with our emotions in healthy ways. Neuroscientists are using it to help people with traumatic brain injuries, post-traumatic stress disorder, ADHD, depression, and anxiety, as well as to ward off dementia. It helps us **STOP** our habitual responses by taking pause and choosing a different course.

I was trained in mindfulness at Vanderbilt University in a two-day class taught by Marc Lesser, who wrote a great book called *Less*. Marc trained with his colleague at Google, Chade-Meng Tan, who wrote the best-selling book on mindfulness called *Search Inside Yourself*. In the seminar, we learned about the benefits of mindfulness and practiced several mindfulness exercises. My favorite was a meditation outside in nature as we walked slowly. The exercise allowed us to experience the world directly through our five senses. It also encouraged us to recognize the thoughts we were having and to label them and the feelings we were having, rather than letting them overpower our thinking.[44]

"Can you sit for one minute and completely quiet your mind? Can you do this without feeling like you're coming out of your skin?"

— Lisa Firestone

Do you find yourself feeling double-minded—a split focus and maybe even guilt—when you are working in the yard on the weekend rather than sitting at the computer working on that big client presentation due on Monday? So-called "mindless" activities can stimulate creativity, so **STOP** beating yourself up and fully engage in whatever you are doing at the moment. Jim Loehr and Tony Swartz ask in "The Making of a Corporate Athlete," "Have you ever suddenly found the solution to a vexing problem while doing something 'mindless' such as jogging, working in the garden, or singing in the shower? That's the left-brain, right-brain shift at work—the fruit of mental oscillation."[45]

Creativity and mental productivity require the ability to get the most out of our brains. The brain has two hemispheres, right and left, with different functions. Left-brain thinking is verbal and analytical. Right-brain thinking is nonverbal and intuitive and uses pictures rather than words.[46] If we use one side of our brain for an extended period of time, it can overheat in a way. Have you ever felt like your brain was fried? Well, that's probably because it was.

Left-right brain oscillation keeps us from getting stuck, suffering from a mental block. If you are stuck and persist further, the solutions you seek may evade you altogether. Making your brain switch between left-brain and right-brain thinking by taking a break for physical activity or concentrating on a hobby you enjoy will help to get those productive juices flowing again. Bonus: It also helps you **STOP** sitting so much. As Daniel Pink writes in his best-selling book, *A Whole New Mind*, those who actively tap into the power of both sides of their brain are better suited for success.[47]

Another way to deliver your brain an effective workout might sound counterintuitive: give your brain a break by unwinding and decompressing. That might mean indulging in a "mindless" activity.

After a long day at work where my mind is engaged for long periods of time, watching a ridiculous sitcom or late-night comedy, with no educational value whatsoever, has therapeutic value. My wife and I like to record the late-night comedy shows and watch the first fifteen minutes at our convenience, because we don't stay up late enough to watch them when they air. We typically skip the interviews with actors pitching their latest movie, but we like the monologues and sketches at the beginning of each show. I think of these short, mindless downtimes as mini vacations. These laugh fests with Sherry release endorphins and stimulate my brain in a different way.

I like what Stuart Heritage wrote on his theguardian.com blog: "Mindlessness operates on the basis that your mind and body already know how to take care of themselves. You don't need to consciously concentrate on your breathing, or what you can smell, because you've unwittingly been doing that since before you were born. To be truly mindless, you need to rely on a combination of snap judgments, uninformed intuition and absent-minded daydreaming. All the things I'm best at, in fact."[48]

Daydreaming, one of my favorite mindless activities, has gotten a bad rap. According to new research, daydreaming can be quite useful despite the repeated warnings of my grade school teachers to focus and pay attention. Does your mind wander? During a class or meeting, do you find yourself staring blankly into space and thinking about what you'll do later in the day, tomorrow, or next week? Psychological research reveals that daydreaming is a strong indicator of an active and well-equipped brain. Take that, Mrs. Estel (my fifth-grade teacher)!

A study published in *Psychological Science* by researchers from the University of Wisconsin and the Max Planck Institute for Human Cognitive and Brain Science suggests that a wandering mind correlates with higher degrees of working memory. Cognitive scientists define this type of memory as the brain's ability to retain and recall information in the face of distractions.[49] Many of our most revered thinkers reported making critically important connections when they were daydreaming. (Maybe daydreaming was part of what got both Edison and Einstein kicked out of elementary school.) So again, it sounds counterintuitive, but daydreaming sharpens your ability to focus.

Ironically, to get the most out of daydreaming, you have to pay attention to the messages your brain is communicating to you. I often come up with my best ideas while I daydream or when I actually dream while sleeping. Keeping a notepad by your bed has long been suggested as a good way to capture your thoughts generated from dreaming, because you otherwise are likely to forget them once you are up and about. Keith Richards famously came up with the opening riff of "I Can't Get No Satisfaction" by recording it when he awoke from a dead sleep. The next morning, he had no memory of it until he noticed the light on his recorder blinking at him.

The takeaway principle is that mindfulness, being conscious and fully present in the moment—even if that moment is daydreaming or laughing at a silly sitcom—lets you tap into the full power of your brain.

Questions for Reflection

- Do you meditate?
- Do you like daydreaming?
- What do you do for downtime?

CHAPTER 5

STOP Claiming Your Baggage

The ability to live in the present moment is a major component of mental wellness.
— *Abraham Maslow*

Do you have any baggage in your life? Are you like me, revisiting the past to claim your baggage? Do you have regrets about the past and wish that you could go back and reverse past mistakes? Do you claim your baggage and drag it with you into the present and, if so, how is that working out for you? Does dwelling on your baggage with your spouse, friends, and family enrich your relationships? I use the term "baggage" to represent our past experiences, mostly negative, which can be debilitating. **STOP** claiming your baggage. It weighs you down.

Examining the past can have therapeutic value if we pull forward fond memories or learn from mistakes. When we look back on our lives and feel nostalgic, we are fondly reflecting on our prior experiences, thus evoking positive emotions. However, from the 1600s through the 1900s, nostalgia was thought to be an undesirable state. In fact, the root of the word nostalgia comes from two Greek words: **nostos**, which means "return home," and **algos**, which means "pain," indicating that it is the suffering evoked by the desire to return to one's place of origin.[50]

In fact, a person who was nostalgic was once viewed as suffering from a neurological disorder. When Swiss doctor Johannes Hoffer first coined the term in 1688, nostalgia was seen as a neurological disease, attributed to demonic causes. Symptoms of nostalgia were thought to include "bouts of weeping, anxiety, irregular heartbeat, anorexia, insomnia, and even smothering sensations."[51] However, since the 1900s, nostalgia has been regarded as a more desirable, positive, and sentimental longing for the past.[52]

Nostalgia may strike when you hear a song from your youth, smell a particular scent in the grocery store, or run into an old friend. When you describe these pleasant memories, you are waxing nostalgic. A study published in *Memory & Cognition* suggests that nostalgia is most strongly associated with our formative years—between the ages of twelve and twenty-two—because that is when we develop our self-image.[53]

Clay Routledge, a researcher at the University of Southampton who studied nostalgia, says, "Nostalgia, then, seems to be one way that people cope with the various negative mental states, or 'psychological threats.' If you're lonely, if you're feeling like a failure, if you feel like you don't know if your life has any purpose [or] if what you're doing has any value, you can reach into this reservoir of nostalgic memories and comfort yourself. We see nostalgia as a psychological resource that people can dip into to conjure up the evidence that they need to assure themselves that they're valued."[54]

Around 800 BC, Homer composed his epic poem *The Odyssey* and with it created one of the most gripping literary accounts of nostalgia. The poem revolves around the adventures of Odysseus who, after emerging victoriously from the Trojan War, embarks on a quest to return to his homeland, the island of Ithaca, and reunite with his faithful wife, Penelope. This quest lasted ten years, seven of which were spent in the possessive arms of the seductive sea nymph Calypso. In an attempt to persuade Calypso to set him free, Odysseus confides to her, "Full well I acknowledge Prudent Penelope cannot compare with your stature of beauty, for she is only a mortal, and you are immortal and ageless. Nevertheless it is she whom I daily desire and pine for. Therefore I long for my home and to see the day of returning."[55] The story of Odysseus is rooted in nostalgia.

Before I get back to the topic of claiming baggage—the nostalgic, good kind as well as the bad kind—permit me to digress to share a favorite nostalgic memory from my days as a student at the University of Illinois that is connected to this fine character, Odysseus.

The Eric Parmenter Odyssey with College Latin

Because I was more interested in sports and girls in high school than academics, I did not take a foreign language, chemistry, or physics. In addition, my high school grades and ACT score were sufficiently low to earn a rejection letter from the University of Illinois (U of I) for freshman admittance. Undaunted and determined to become a physician, I enrolled in the local community college, Parkland College, where I earned straight As and an associate's degree in biology. I transferred to the U of I as a junior. However, I still lacked chemistry, physics, and a foreign language, so I was required to complete those courses during my junior or senior year. To fulfill the language requirement, I enrolled in an introductory Latin class because most medical terms have their roots in Latin.

I signed up for Latin 101 and struggled all semester under Professor Deming as we translated Homer's *Odyssey* from Latin into English. I finished with a C. I struggled even more with Latin 201 and dropped out of the class after a few weeks. Meanwhile, chemistry and physics were too challenging for my right-brain orientation, so I dropped out of those classes, too. I decided that if being a doctor required mostly a left-brain orientation, then I was not cut out to have MD after my name. I changed my major to psychology and thoroughly enjoyed classes like abnormal psychology, where we were assigned reading such as *One Flew Over the Cuckoo's Nest*.

My senior year arrived, and I sat down with my academic advisor to determine the courses I needed to complete my psychology degree. He reminded me that though my major had changed, the requirement to complete a fourth-level foreign language remained. How did this slip my mind? I guess I suppressed the not-so-distant bad memory of dropping out of Latin. "But wait!" I exclaimed to my academic advisor. "Did you say that I must complete a fourth-level foreign language course, not all four levels?"

He said, "No one has ever asked that question, because in order to pass a fourth-level course you must have mastered levels one, two, and three, and you barely passed level one and did not take two or three."

"Please check your manual," I insisted, "because if it doesn't require me to take all levels but to only pass the highest level, then I will enroll in Latin 401."

He double-checked and agreed that if I passed level four and my remaining classes, I would earn my degree. He agreed to this plan with the stern warning that I was taking a big risk.

I enrolled in Latin 401 with the same Professor Deming I had for 101 and 201. He seemed surprised to see me. Imagine that. He instructed the class that in this advanced Latin class there would be no quizzes, no midterm, and no papers. The class grade would be based entirely on the final exam. We would study Homer's second great book, *The Iliad*, all semester and he would hand out a Latin version of one chapter (called books) of *The Iliad* as the final exam. The exam would require us to translate the chapter of his choosing from Latin into English. We would not know until the moment the exam was handed out which chapter he would assign.

I struggled mightily all semester. Basically, I was lost, but I hung in until the end. We had one week from the end of class to prepare for the final exam. There was no way I could translate any chapter of *The Iliad* from Latin to English. I decided to pick one chapter, the one I thought he spent the most time on during class. For that entire week, I painstakingly memorized Book III of *The Iliad* in English.

The day of the final exam came. There were only about twenty students in the class, and we all sat anxiously waiting for the professor to hand out the final exam. Much to my delight and relief, he handed out Book III. All of the other students did what one does when translating. They looked at the Latin words and wrote down an English rendering, back and forth, for three hours. Not me! There was no need to look at the Latin words at all because I did not know what they meant. I just started writing Book III from memory in English. And so I began . . .

> *When the companies were thus arrayed, each under its own captain,*
> *the Trojans advanced as a flight of wild fowl or cranes that scream*
> *overhead when rain and winter drive them over the flowing waters*
> *of Oceanus to bring death and destruction on the Pygmies, and they*
> *wrangle in the air as they fly; but the Achaeans marched silently,*
> *in high heart, and minded to stand by one another.*

I finished in less than an hour, way ahead of the other students, and learned a week later I had passed with an A! I graduated from the U of I with a bachelor's degree in psychology and a book of *The Iliad* memorized.

Even as I write these words, I feel nostalgic. My family asks me to tell this story to new family members from time to time. I sometimes wake up in a cold sweat from a nightmare that I did not graduate and my whole life has been a fraud. Oh well, I am not going to claim that baggage.

We all make mistakes, we all have regrets, and we all have things that we wish we could do over. In golf, if you strike a ball badly you can elect to use a "mulligan" and try again. In the classic 1980s movie *Back to the Future*, Marty McFly journeys back in time to fix the mistakes of his dysfunctional family. He succeeds in the nick of time with the help of a nutty professor and a DeLorean sports-car time machine. Life offers few mulligans, and unfortunately, to my knowledge, nobody's invented a time machine.

So how should you deal with your baggage? Look at your past mistakes briefly and systematically with the goal of learning from them. That is the only reason to ever examine the contents of your old baggage—to make sure you don't repeat your biggest bloopers.

Here are a few steps to help you unpack and ditch your negative baggage:

- Embrace your humanity. We are all flawed human beings who make mistakes.
- Forgive yourself and others. Reconciliation is good medicine.
- Remember that you can't un-ring the bell. The past can't be changed.
- For deep wounds from the past, secure the help of a professional therapist.
- Embrace the road ahead. You are gifted and have much to offer now and in the future.

Another perspective on baggage is to leverage the baggage of your greatest weakness, your disadvantages, your Achilles' heel, into your greatest strength.

Achilles, a character from Greek mythology, finds his way into the *Iliad* adventure. When Achilles was a baby, it was foretold that he would die young. His mother Thetis took Achilles to the River Styx, which was supposed to offer powers of invulnerability, and she dipped his body into the water to prevent his death. But because Thetis held Achilles by the heel, the magical river water never touched it. Achilles grew up to be a man of war who survived many great battles but was ultimately killed by a poisonous arrow that pierced the only weakness in his body, the heel that was not washed in the River Styx.[56] This is how we got the phrase "Achilles' heel," which alludes to our greatest weakness.

In Malcolm Gladwell's masterful book *David and Goliath*, the author describes, through a serious of compelling stories, how underdogs and misfits have turned the baggage of deep tragedy, disabilities, and weaknesses into their greatest strengths. My Achilles' heel, since the time I was a small boy, was that I was considered dumb and weak. I could not read very well and was assigned to the slow-readers group in the first grade. My first grade teacher used names of birds to separate readers into groups based on their reading ability. The Cardinals were the best readers, followed by the Blue Jays. I was in the third and last group, the Robins. Putting labels on small children can be devastating. Everyone knew that a robin is more like a mud hen, and that the Robins were the dumb kids.

I was equally bad at math, and my handwriting was poor. I struggled all through grade school, junior high, and high school until my senior year when I turned things around with newfound purpose and got straight As. But my Herculean effort proved too little, too late to earn admission to the University of Illinois, so I enrolled in the local community college after receiving my rejection letter.

I love athletics and enjoyed playing all kinds of sports as a kid. Unfortunately, I was never good enough to earn a starting position on a team. I was usually the kid who came off the bench late in the game once the outcome had been determined. My brother Todd, who is two and a half years older than I am and my constant playmate as a kid, was fast, strong, and a natural athlete. He could hit with a tremendous force and knock you down. He could grip your hand until it hurt. Believe me, I was knocked down more than a few times by him but was always grateful when he came to my defense against bullies who often pushed me around.

I eventually cut the baggage loose and turned my weaknesses into strengths. I learned to be a good listener to compensate for being such a poor reader. My father, who is a preacher, captivated my attention through his sermons. At Sunday lunch with the family after church, we would discuss the sermon, whether it was my father's or a visiting preacher's, in great detail and further dissect the sermon. I rarely took detailed notes during a lecture because I find it distracting, and I still don't today. Instead, I've trained myself to listen intently, and this skill served me well in college lectures and in my career as a salesperson, consultant, and manager.

I spent many hours driving all over the state of Illinois in my early career in sales and benefits-consulting and would listen to books on tape for hours at a time. I looked forward to the long drives because it allowed me to listen to great books.

I also excelled at public speaking. Because I was disadvantaged in most things academic, I developed a quick wit, which I used as a weapon against my brother's superior physical strength. He could hit me with his fist, but I could take him out with a well-timed and strategically delivered insult. I used my sharp wit with my grade-school teachers, which did not enhance my report card.

In high school, however, one of the few classes I enjoyed and excelled in was speech. Ironically, I was painfully shy socially but could stand up in front of an audience and deliver a well-designed speech and received great praise from Mr. Keith Page, my high school speech teacher who was also the weatherman on the local Channel 15 news.

Finally, I turned my weakness in reading into a love for writing. How ironic that I can write much better than I can read. Writing is a word-by-word, thought-by-thought exercise that is forgiving. I can write a word, erase it, try a different word, cut and paste a section to a different location. I can make many mistakes and fix them later. I enjoy telling stories verbally and in writing. I generally earned As on term papers in high school and college. My father would read them and correct the grammar, and we would discuss the content together like we dissected a sermon after church.

Early in my career I started writing articles in my field of employee benefits and healthcare and was delighted to have many of these articles accepted for publication. I was not required to write articles. I did it for fun and to earn some credibility. Of course, I had opportunities to work with editors to clean up my mistakes, just as they did on the words you are reading right now.

In *David and Goliath*, Gladwell tells stories of a highly successful options trader, Gary Cohn, who overcame his dyslexia by taking risks and eventually became the CEO of Goldman Sachs, and David Bois who overcame his dyslexia by skipping college, going straight to law school, and making it through by finely honed listening skills to become one of the most successful litigators in the country. These men and many other people have learned to compensate for their greatest weakness and turned it into their greatest strength.

I do not know if dyslexia is my issue with reading. It might be, but I turned my weaknesses in reading and athletics into strengths in listening, coaching, teaching, writing, and speaking. I have hired actuaries to do the math. I took the valuables out of the old suitcases and let go of the baggage covered with labels like "weak" and "dumb."

There is a unique retail store way off the beaten path in Scottsboro, Alabama, called Unclaimed Baggage. This store takes up an entire city block in this small town and sells baggage that people have left on airplanes and in airports. You can find almost anything there at a great price. In 1970, Doyle Owens headed to Washington, DC, with an idea, a borrowed pickup truck, and a three-hundred-dollar loan to pick up his first load of unclaimed baggage. He sold the contents on card tables in an old rented house. The venture was an instant success.[57]

Why do we have so much interest in our baggage, and, for that matter, other people's baggage? Why do we claim baggage that is of no apparent value?

In a psychological sense, our baggage is the negative experiences from the past that we all too often claim. People claim baggage for multiple reasons. We view the past with 20/20 clarity, which has an addictive allure because the brain is not comfortable with the uncertainty of the future. Revisiting the past can be a guilty pleasure for some. Other folks revisit the past because they haven't found closure yet and find it difficult to move beyond regrets. Others have success barriers, rooted in low self-esteem, and do not feel entitled to positive experiences, so dwelling on a negative past allows them to spend time in a place that is perversely comfortable. Self-sabotage leads you to keep dragging your baggage with you no matter how heavy it is.[58]

If you are stuck in self-sabotage mode, you may want to find a practitioner of neuro-emotional technique (http://www.netmindbody.com), which uses a noninvasive process to identify and clear past emotional traumas that may be affecting your ability to move forward.

Whatever the reason, dwelling on the past is harmful for our health, according to researchers at Ohio University. This study found a physiological link between inflammation and dwelling on negative incidents.[59] Inflammation has been linked to a number of disorders including cardiovascular disease, diabetes, and depression.[60]

Knowing which bags to leave in the past, where they belong, and which ones to retrieve for your future journey requires skill. I am a great admirer of the genius of the architect Frank Lloyd Wright. Wright had a lot of baggage but had the uncanny skill of knowing what to leave behind. His commitment to not looking back was so staunch that he had the rear window removed from his 1940 Cherokee Red Lincoln Continental. When asked about it, he claimed he never looked back, only forward.[61] **STOP** claiming your baggage and letting it hold you back.

Frank Lloyd Wright's Customized 1940 Lincoln Continental

Questions for Reflection

- Do have regrets or experiences that you have a difficult time leaving in the past?
- What are you nostalgic about?
- What are some of the most important lessons that you have learned in life the hard way?

CHAPTER 6

STOP the Clutter

Out of clutter find simplicity.
—Albert Einstein

Are you surrounded by clutter? Some folks don't mind or even claim to prefer living with dirty clothes on the floor, dirty dishes in the sink, stacks of papers all over their desk, and food wrappers and pop cans lying around. What about the garage, attic, and closets full of stuff you never use but might need someday? Really? Have you used it in the past year or is it a valuable keepsake? You may be like Maggie Stiefvater, who says,

---

"Clutter is my natural habitat."

— *Maggie* Stiefvater, The Scorpio Races

Peter Walsh, an organizational expert and former host of The Learning Channel's *Clean Sweep*, divides clutter into two general types. "Memory" clutter is stuff that reminds us of important events, like old school programs or newspaper clippings. "Someday" clutter refers to items you won't toss because you feel you might need them someday.[62]

I am an admitted neat freak. My motto is: "A place for everything and everything in its place." I find it hard to concentrate on my work surrounded by clutter. In college, I had to clean my room before I could sit down and study. True, some of that behavior was procrastination, but for me, a cluttered environment leads to a cluttered mind. Maybe I am too easily distracted. But I know myself. I need to remove as many distractions as possible from my field of view to be able to properly focus.

My mother taught us to keep our rooms clean, and we had to pass her inspection before we could move on. I guess her teaching stuck and maybe that's why if I fail to **STOP** the clutter, I hear her voice and worry that my space won't pass inspection, and I won't be able to go out and play.

I am not talking about hoarding, which is clutter on steroids. Compulsive hoarding is commonly considered to be a type of obsessive compulsive disorder (OCD). Some estimate that as many as one in four people with OCD also are compulsive hoarders. Recent research suggests that nearly one in five compulsive hoarders have nonhoarding OCD symptoms. Compulsive hoarding is considered a feature of OCD that may develop along with other mental illnesses, such as dementia and schizophrenia.[63] Please seek professional help if you suffer from OCD and related hoarding, because this book won't deliver the help you need.

In this chapter, I am referring to the run-of-the-mill messiness that produces stress.

Why do we have clutter in our lives—not just papers on the desk—but messy relationships and unfulfilled commitments? One reason: lapsing into the habit of procrastination. We all procrastinate at times. I cleaned my college room to procrastinate doing my homework. Some leave clutter around to procrastinate the unpleasant work of cleaning.

A major reason that we get paralyzed in the mess is fear of change. Some people stay in unhealthy relationships because of lack of confidence and fear of the alternative. They at least know what they have, as unpleasant as it may be, but fear the unknown. Some think that shoving the clutter in a drawer or tote is dealing with the mess. Out of sight, out of mind. Stashing your clutter out of sight is merely avoiding the reality, whether a messy house or a toxic dump of a relationship. If this applies to you, ask yourself: *What is it that you are avoiding by failing to deal with or purge the messy stuff, organize your space and life, and get on with positive behavior?*

Another reason we may have clutter in our lives is that we live in a society that places high value on stuff. We are bombarded by advertising that lures us with the message that our lives would be better if only we had the product being pitched. Complexity rather than simplicity rules the day. I appreciate now, more than ever, the 1981 book *Freedom of Simplicity* written by my parents' dear friend, Richard Foster, who wrote, "Contemporary culture is plagued by the passion to possess. The unreasoned boast abounds that the good life is found in accumulation, that 'more is better.' Indeed, we often accept this notion without question, with the result that the lust for affluence in contemporary society has become psychotic: it has completely lost touch with reality."[64]

Clutter may even be making you fat, says Walsh, who wrote *Does This Clutter Make My Butt Look Fat?* Working on his show, he noticed an association between the amount of clutter people have and their excess weight. He says that the common denominator is a life of consumption—too much stuff, too much to eat.[65] When you declutter your home, start with the pantry. Getting rid of the unhealthy processed food will not only streamline your environment and help you get organized, but may also help you drop a few unwanted pounds. You may also find the courage to deal with your messy relationship as you ditch the clutter in your surroundings. There is a direct correlation between the two.

People who ask professionals to help them declutter their home or office often admit that they feel overwhelmed and complain about the difficulty of finding things. Many people with health problems such as asthma are living in cluttered environments where dust and pet dander are contributing to or exacerbating their health problems.

One of my health system clients, as part of its population health business, instituted a Complex Care management program. This program identifies people in a population through stratification of multiple sources of individual data (health and pharmacy claims, biometric screening and lab results, self-reported health assessment data, etc.) and then reaches out to offer a comprehensive care plan with the support of:

- a primary care physician,
- a care advisor,
- a social worker,
- a dietician,
- a pharmacist, and
- a nurse.

Most of these patients are suffering from multiple diseases and ailments (we call them "multiple comorbidities" in healthcare jargon). Not only are they suffering from complex health problems, they often suffer from depression and behavioral health issues as well. Making matters worse, they are being bounced around the healthcare and insurance "system." I use system in quotes because it is more often the lack of a system.

The folks targeted for this program often wound up making frequent trips to the emergency room and not getting the kind of help that they truly need. The combination of poor health and a dysfunctional healthcare system results in large and unnecessary healthcare costs that are typically paid by their employer once the patient has met all their deductibles and co-payments.

With that as background, here is the story about a family that needed Complex Care support. The father worked as a janitor at the hospital and the mother was unemployed. The couple had twin girls of grade-school age who suffered from severe allergies and asthma, among other things, and ended up in the emergency room several times a year. The mother suffered from numerous health problems as well, and all of the family members were depressed.

Once the family was identified, they were invited to participate in the Complex Care program. The program included the waiving of their deductibles and co-payments and provided far more resources than are normally covered by insurance. Of course, the employer is motivated to get out-of-control costs under control, so the program is a win-win. It removes the out-of-pocket costs for the family, an immediate benefit, and helps the family achieve a better quality of life and improved health, which lowers the cost for the employer.

The family accepted the invitation and a care team was assembled. The team pulled medical records as far back as they could find and conducted a complete set of physical exams and tests for each member of the family. They conducted interviews and counseling sessions and completed one of the most important and often neglected steps in medicine today, a home visit.

Until you understand someone's environment, you really do not have a complete picture of their lives. Upon visiting the home, the social worker discovered that the house was a disastrous mess with dust and dander from the family's five cats. The team approved payment for a housecleaning service and some environmental training, and they talked to the family about the cats. The family decided that the cats were actually part of the problem, so they volunteered to let the team find a new home for their pets. The trips to the ER went away, and the quality of health and life improved. The entire family's depression lifted and was replaced with newfound joy. Yes, the health plan spent some extra money on these services but in the long run this intervention saved thousands of dollars on avoidable medical expenses. More importantly, the family enjoyed a higher quality of life and less stress.

I encourage you to think about clutter for a moment. Are you a neat freak like me? If so, why? Is it the voice of your mother in your head or a procrastination behavior? Maybe you need to lighten up a bit? I think my family would say that I could benefit by taking it down a notch or two. Not every child of ours shares my passion for neatness. I won't name any names, but there is more than one kid who doesn't quite share my values on neatness.

Are you a clutter bug? If so, why? Are you avoiding something that needs attention? Have you ever thought about this at all?

Sherry and I have downsized our home by about half and as a result of less space, have purged quite a bit of stuff. Neither of us is a hoarder, but despite both of us tending far more toward neatness, we found many things were just not necessary. We packed away some keepsakes in a few totes, and we donated a number of loads of good things that we just didn't need to charity. We sold some furniture and other items and made some extra cash by doing so. We have greatly simplified our lives and it feels good. Everyone should move at least once every ten years, if for no other reason than to force you to purge. We now enjoy more free time and less worry and stress.

So take some time to reflect. What is your relationship to clutter? If clutter is creating stress for you, **STOP** the clutter.

Questions for Reflection

- Are you a neat freak, clutter bug, or somewhere in between?
- What clutter do you have in your life that needs to be purged?
- What do you think your physical environment is telling you about your personality?

CHAPTER 7

STOP Your Worst Habit

The key to exercising regularly, losing weight, raising exceptional children, becoming more productive, building revolutionary companies and social movements, and achieving success is understanding how habits work.

—*Charles Duhigg,* The Power of Habit

According to most economics textbooks, human beings are super-rational creatures who know what is in their own best interest and always act accordingly. This is called the rational agent model, which is a central tenet in the field of economics. If this is true, why do we buy things we don't need, and why do we do things that are not in our best interest? On a micro level, why did I eat raw cookie dough every afternoon my junior and senior year in college?

While the rational agent model is useful for economic analysis when we examine the economy as a whole, it clearly does not correspond to how human beings behave in the real world. So why do people sometimes make decisions that are not strictly in their own best interest? Nowhere is irrational behavior more evident than in the study of habits. Many of us have, or have had, a least one irrational bad habit that is so deeply engrained that it seems impossible to break. But you can find the strength to **STOP** your worst habit.

Behavioral economics is a relatively recent field of study, which examines how nonrational factors like emotion or altruism influence economic choices. It also helps us understand other choices about health and habits. It applies the lessons of disciplines like psychology and sociology to explain decisions about consumption, investment, and other facets of economic life and human behavior. "Choice Architecture" is the positioning of choices in such a way as to influence the decision in the direction that the "Choice Architect" believes to be in the best interest of the decision maker.

Whether or not we know it, we are all Choice Architects. Choice Architecture, popularized in the book *Nudge* by Richard Thaler and Cass Sunstein, provides practical examples of how you can change the world for the better by leveraging behavioral economic principles.[66] An example of acting as a Choice Architect is arranging your pantry to put the healthiest foods, like almonds, at eye level and less healthy food on a shelf where you won't see it, or removing the unhealthy food altogether from your pantry.

Kyra Bobinet, MD, MPH, tells a story from her own life in her book *Well Designed Life* about how she became motivated to redesign her refrigerator. She observed her colleague, Dr. BJ Fogg, director of the Persuasive Tech Lab at Stanford University, set a few clear glass containers in front of the participants in a team meeting. The containers were full of bright red strawberries and snap peas, and he instructed the team to dig in and enjoy the healthy food from his garden. Krya rearranged the layout of the food in her fridge as a result as a way to change the snacking behaviors of her family. She put healthy colorful food in clear containers at eye level in the front of the fridge, switched the chocolate chip cookies to oatmeal raisin, and put them in the bottom of the freezer. After iterating (a key design principle from her book) on this method a few times, she began to notice the intended change in her family's, and her own, snacking habits. The healthy food was easy to see and readily available; the unhealthy food was either gone or out of sight. This is a great practical example of Choice Architecture.

In my master of business administration (MBA) program at the University of Chicago Booth School of Business, I had the privilege of taking a behavioral economics class in London that was taught by Richard H.

Thaler, director of the Center for Decision Research and codirector (with Robert Shiller) of the Behavioral Economics Project at the National Bureau of Economic Research. One of the key ideas that stuck with me from this field of study is the idea of the timing of rewards.

Think about rewards. When I was a college student, there was a store called The Cookie Dough Factory directly across the street from the psychology building where I had many of my classes. I formed a habit of frequenting this shop every afternoon after class and ordering a cup of white-chocolate, macadamia-nut cookie dough. I'd sit outside, enjoying my sweet treat and the sunshine, for about thirty minutes before I moved on to other activities.

That behavior produced an immediate reward. The taste of the soft cookie dough, white chocolate, and macadamia nut in my mouth was delightful. That delicious taste, the satiation of my hunger, and the pickup from sugar combined for my reward. However, there were less obvious rewards too. I had finished several hours of sitting in consecutive classes, and this was a break from the monotony. I enjoyed sitting outside, getting some fresh air, and clearing my mind. That transition time from work to play and then dinner before I sat down again for a long evening of study was rewarding as well.

The benefits of not eating cookie dough are obvious: raw eggs mixed with sugar and flour and chocolate are not healthy. Sluggishness could easily set in and eventual weight gain could result. I did not care about that at the time because the rewards of optimal energy and weight maintenance were not immediate. All I cared about was my daily cup of sugary sweet deliciousness. I admit it also helped that I was active athletically in college, so I quickly burned off my not-so-healthy diet. I have always had a sweet tooth and still crave a midafternoon snack, but now I reach for some almonds or a fruit smoothie.

Habits are linked to cues, behaviors, and rewards. We often receive an immediate reward from acting on habits. When I came out of that psychology building at the U of I, I was leaving classes where we studied the teachings of people like B. F. Skinner. Skinner taught us the difference between *immediate* vs. *delayed reinforcement*. Immediate reinforcement occurs immediately after desired or undesired behavior occurs. This type of reinforcement has the strongest and quickest effect in controlling behavior. The longer the delay, the less likely the learning. At the time, I didn't make the connection between what I was learning in class and my afternoon cookie dough, but I was receiving immediate reinforcement.

So what habit do you have that is irrational and perhaps unhealthy? Is it smoking, overeating, impulsive spending, drinking too much, or watching too much TV? How do you break bad habits and form new ones? Charles Duhigg, the leading author on habits, provides deep insight into how habits are linked to rewards. I think of changing habits as a form of Choice Architecture. I encourage you to study Duhigg's writings for a deeper and more comprehensive dive, but here are some basic concepts boiled down from Duhigg's classic book *The Power of Habit* to help you design new environments or routines in order to break bad habits.[67]

Identify your craving. What craving is powering your habit? Once you identify your craving, you can begin to think about cues and rewards associated with this craving. For instance, Claude Hopkins tried to sell Pepsodent toothpaste in the late 1920s by creating a craving loop. He described the plaque on teeth as "the film" and positioned advertising to say "Just run your tongue across your teeth, you'll feel a film—that's what makes your teeth look 'off color' and invites decay." Another ad featured smiling beauties and proclaimed: "Note how many pretty teeth are seen everywhere, millions are using a new method of teeth cleaning. Why would any woman have dingy film on her teeth? Pepsodent removes the film!"

These advertisements relied on a cue—tooth film—that everyone experiences and is hard to ignore. Telling someone to run their tongue across their teeth worked as a cue. Do it now. How does it feel? Do you need to brush your teeth?

The reward was positioned as the result of brushing your teeth—with Pepsodent, of course. This reward included the way you were trained by the advertising to perceive that using Pepsodent to brush your teeth would cause others to perceive you as more attractive. Here is the example of Pepsodent that Duhigg provides in his model for all habits, called the "Habit Loop":

Pit Stop for Habit-Loop Tune-Up[68]

"Tune Up"

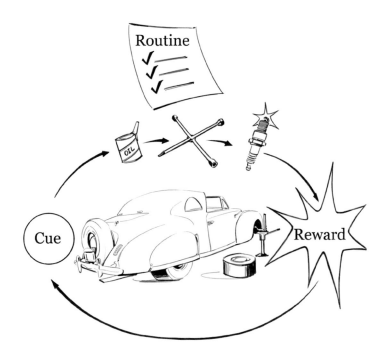

The above illustration is based upon the work of
Charles Duhigg in his book *The Power of Habit*.
Used with permission by Penguin Random House Publishers New York.

This Habit Loop can be created for any habit. Identify the cue, the routine the cue produces, and the reward, which in turn reinforces the cue. Cues can be changed and rewards altered, but that will not break the habit. If you have a habit of obsessively looking at your smartphone during meetings, turning it to Do Not Disturb may temporarily remove the cue to check your phone. However, that action will not necessarily break the habit, because the next time the phone is turned on, you will respond to the cue in the same way.

Some rewards come in the form of altered brain chemistry, like the result of smoking a cigarette or drinking alcohol. Failure to break these habits can be devastating, but we all know from watching people smoke, even when they are dying from lung cancer, that breaking them is difficult.

According to Duhigg, the **Golden Rule of habit change is to keep the old cue, deliver the old reward, but insert a new routine**. If you use the same cue and reward, you can shift the routine and change the habit. This Golden Rule has influenced treatments for many destructive behaviors, but if your habits are severely ingrained, you may need the guidance of a professional as you rebuild your routines.

What is your worst habit? Analyze the cues, routines, and rewards of that habit and think about how you can replace the routines based on the same cues and rewards. It will take time to break an old habit. Willpower is never strong enough to achieve sustained results. I cannot cover the entire complex process of breaking bad habits in this chapter, so I recommend reading *The Power of Habit*.

Let's go back to my example of the habit of eating cookie dough after class. Much of the reward was a break from the exhaustion of sitting through class with a high level of mental concentration and the release of stress that came from letting my mind wander while sitting outside and enjoying the campus. I could have had a fruit smoothie, sat outside, enjoyed the campus and experienced much of the same reward in response to the same stimulus. Again, the key is not to change the cues or the rewards, but the routine in between. Give it a try.

I offer some caution here that your habits may be more serious than indulging in eating cookie dough every day. If you are trying to break a long-held bad habit, your bad stress may go up for a while as you build new routines. For example, if you end your evening with a nightcap or two or three, your sleep will be interrupted. When you switch your nightly routine to brewing a nice cup of hot chamomile tea, you'll likely miss your alcohol for a while. However, once you put a **STOP** to your worst habit, your bad stress will eventually go down and emotions of joy will be evoked in new ways. Your long-term reward will be sweet. You will experience new freedom and a greater sense of well-being.

Questions for Reflection

- What is your worst habit?
- What have you done, if anything, to break that habit?
- What ways could you change the routines of this habit without changing the cues or rewards?

CHAPTER 8

STOP Working on Low Priorities

"Mr. Carnegie," Taylor said. "I would advise you to make a list of the ten most important things you can do. And then, start doing number one." And, the story goes, a week later Taylor received a check for $10,000.
— *Richard Rumelt,* Good Strategy, Bad Strategy

Are you like me? Do you have an endless list of things to do? My memory is not strong enough to remember all the important things to do, so I need to write them down. I use an organizational app that syncs with multiple devices, which contains multiple categories of my to-do lists. I have a list called Eric's Today List, Financial, Bucket List, Groceries, etc.

To-do lists are great. They keep us organized and ensure that we don't forget to follow through on commitments. The problem is not the lists or the number of things on our list, but how we prioritize our focus and energy. The quote above is from a famous story in which Andrew Carnegie, the Pittsburgh steel magnate and richest man in the world in the mid- to late 1800s, inquired of Frederick Taylor, an efficiency expert, on how to become more effective. The brilliance in Taylor's advice was not making a list of the most important things but starting with No. 1.[69] Deciding on your No. 1 most important thing to do, with the understanding that you will then invest the majority of your time doing one activity, forces you to reflect on your priorities.

I developed a method early in my career that I continue to follow to this day. It was inspired by the Carnegie-Taylor story but I am not certain where I learned it. Some of the great books that I read in my early twenties included *Think and Grow Rich* by Napoleon Hill, *How to Win Friends and Influence People* by Dale Carnegie, *The Prophet* by Kahlil Gibran, and *The 7 Habits of Highly Effective People* by Stephen R. Covey. This method might have been a combination of things I learned from those books:

1. Make a list of important things to do the next day before this day ends or early in the morning of each day.
2. Reorder the list with the No. 1 priority at the top, No. 2 next, and continue in descending order.
3. Decide if any of the tasks can be eliminated, delegated, or delayed and either cross them off the list, move the date out, or take some time asking your delegate to complete the task.
4. Finally, begin working on your No. 1 priority and get as far into it as you can before moving on to No. 2.

Of this list, No. 4 is the most important step, but it starts with determining your most important priority and then forces you to focus on that priority, to the exclusion of all the others, if necessary. The goal is not to accomplish as much of your list as you can in a day, as rewarding as that may be, but to make meaningful headway on your top priorities, sticking to the order of priority you've assigned each to-do. If all you do today is make meaningful progress on your most important priority, even without completing it, you have used your time wisely.

Although this method has produced fantastic results for me, it has always been difficult to execute. It has become more difficult over the years as I work in more distracting environments. Open floor plans in offices and the proliferation of digital devices that call out for attention and increased demands on my time make this level of focus challenging. I will admit that I am not able to do this every day, but when I do, I accomplish much more. Incidentally, I rarely face criticism for not completing something of lesser importance when I am focused on my most important priorities.

Setting aside time in the week to follow up on e-mails and other tasks helps keep me more focused during the rest of the time. Reviewing my calendar at the beginning and end of each week and eliminating meetings, setting aside preparation times, and prioritizing work as part of our Corporate Performance Athlete initiative at work fits right into this method.

We work in teams in my company and that involves many meetings, conference calls, and frequent coordination with colleagues and clients. I have found that sharing my top priorities with my team and my clients, as my boss does with his team, serves multiple aims.

First, it lets everyone on my team know where my priorities are and how I plan to spend the majority of my time. Others give me more grace when I do not complete other tasks that are not high priority, because my team understands the importance of focus. Second, it allows team members to align their priorities and workflow with mine, so that we are all working on high priorities. Third, while the priorities of each individual differ, my priorities are aligned with those of my boss and his with corporate objectives, and my team's priorities are aligned with mine. The result? We reach most of our goals and see the impact of our work.

What would your day be like if your to-do list was shortened and more meaningful? Would you have more energy? Andrew Carnegie said, "The men who have succeeded are men who have chosen one line and stuck to it."[70] The broad application of this saying, to me, is not that we only have one career in life, but that we will accomplish more by deliberately choosing what *not* to do, in life, in a career, or educational pursuit. Having your key priority top of mind allows you to sharply focus each day.

Hyrum Smith, cofounder of Franklin Covey, said, "When your daily activities are in concert with your highest priorities, you have a credible claim to inner peace."[71] Therefore, when you **STOP** focusing on low priorities, you'll find that your schedule yields less stress, evokes more joy, and allows you to achieve greater well-being and higher personal performance.

Questions for Reflection

- What are your top three priorities right now?
- How much time do you spend on priorities, other than your top three, on average per day?
- What things do you spend time on that, if eliminated altogether, would evoke greater well-being?

CHAPTER 9

STOP Setting Too Many Dumb Goals

If you don't know where you're going, you'll end up somewhere else.

—*Yogi Berra*

Do you set personal or work goals? I have set goals for many years and sometimes those goals have been **D.U.M.B.**, because they

- **D**on't
- **U**p
- **M**y
- **B**ehavior

Here are some examples of D.U.M.B. goals:

- Goals that are too many in number (more than ten).
- Goals that are vague, like "Lose weight."
- Goals that can't easily be measured, like "Be nicer to people."
- Goals that do not require action.
- Goals that are unrealistic, like "Increase sales by 200 percent."
- Goals that do not have a timeline for completion.

In other words, goals that **D**on't **U**p **M**y **B**ehavior are indeed dumb, because they are the opposite of **S.M.A.R.T.** goals that are:

- **S**pecific
- **M**easurable
- **A**ctionable
- **R**ealistic
- **T**ime-bound

I used to create big binders with my goals for the year and for life and spend lots of time developing my goals. I am extremely goal-oriented, but sometimes I get carried away. One of my past mistakes was having way too many goals.

If you were asked to list your goals and could not do it from memory, you likely have too many. The fewer the better, as far as I am concerned. You are far better off having three goals for the year that really matter to you and to achieve all three than to have twenty-five and achieve fewer than half.

Related to the number of goals is the wordiness of the goals.

Example A: Lose ten pounds by May 1 by working out four days a week for 30 minutes daily and eliminating red meat and alcohol. Bonus points: this is relatively short and sweet.

Example B: Engage in moderate-intensity cardiorespiratory exercise training for 30 minutes or more five days per week or more for a total of at least 150 minutes per week, vigorous-intensity cardiorespiratory exercise training for at least 20 minutes or more for three days per week, perform resistance exercises for each of the major muscle groups, and neuromotor exercise involving balance, agility, and coordination, and complete flexibility exercises for each of the major muscle-tendon groups on two or more days.

Which of these two goals are you more likely to remember? Goal A, of course. Goal A is S.M.A.R.T.

- **S**pecific: Lose ten pounds—not just lose weight.

- **M**easurable: A simple bathroom scale will provide the necessary data.

- **A**ctionable: Work out four days weekly for thirty minutes and eliminate red meat and alcohol.

- **R**ealistic: If you start in January and, assuming you have excess weight to lose, ten pounds in five months is achievable.

- **T**ime-bound: May 1 is a deadline.

In fact, Goal B is not even a goal. It is a process to achieve a goal. A common mistake is mixing up goals and the process to achieve them.

Our society is obsessed with goal setting, particularly "stretch goals" that may not be realistic. For instance, in the early 2000s, General Motors set a goal to achieve 29 percent market share of the US auto market. The company even had pins printed up for employees to wear that said "29."[72] Not only did GM *not* reach its goal, the US government spent about $50 billion to bailout GM as a result of the company's 2009 bankruptcy.[73]

Goals should stretch us, or they are not goals. Losing one pound in five months is not a stretch goal. For most people, their weight fluctuates that much from one day to the next. But goals that are unrealistic are not stretch goals either. A good stretch goal must be actionable and achievable.

A Harvard Business School report called *Goals Gone Wild* claims that "goal setting has been treated like an over-the-counter medication when it should really be treated with more care, as a prescription-strength medication."[74] The report points out that goal setting can have a number of unintended consequences, such as:

- focusing attention too much or on the wrong things that can lead people to participate in extreme behaviors to achieve the goals;

- an overly narrow focus that neglects non-goal areas;

- a rise in unethical behavior;

- distorted risk preferences;

- corrosion of organizational culture; and
- reduced intrinsic motivation.[75]

So keep it real. Keep it simple. **STOP** setting dumb goals, which are either too easily forgotten or worse, add bad stress and foster unhealthy behavior.

Questions for Reflection

- Do you have more than ten goals?
- Are your goals S.M.A.R.T.?
- What goals, that if removed or changed, would enhance your well-being?

CHAPTER 10

STOP Your Smartphone Addiction

With great power comes great responsibility, however, and scientists are starting to learn that spending so much time staring at our phones is actually doing some damage to our physical, social and intellectual lives.

—K. Thor Jensen

The twenty-first-century era in which we live is more technologically advanced and sophisticated than any time in history. The world is getting smaller in the sense that we can travel across the globe quickly and communicate with people all over the world instantaneously. We conduct business in a global economy. We are relentlessly flooded by messages on our smartphones, bombarded with sounds and images on our flat screen HDTVs, and inundated by the electronic clutter of multimedia.

Some millennials and older folks may remember when facsimile (fax) machines hit the market in the 1980s. If you are from Generation Z (born after 1995),[76] you may have only heard about fax machines. A fax machine was a clunky piece of electronic equipment that plugged into a phone jack on the wall (another dinosaur) that allowed you to insert a written document into your machine and send it to someone else who had a fax machine. The receiving machine would produce a copy, a facsimile, of the same document on warm paper accompanied by a very loud screeching noise. By the way, Generation Z, a phone jack is a special outlet in a wall into which you plugged a wire from your phone, enabling it to transmit a voice signal carried over phone wires. Weird stuff, huh?

The Generation Names Based on Date of Birth

Generation Name	Births Starting	Births Ending	Youngest Age in 2016	Oldest Age in 2016
The Lost Generation- The Generation of 1914	1890	1915	101	126
The Interbellum Generation	1901	1913	103	115
The Greatest Generation	1910	1925	91	106
The Silent Generation	1923	1944	72	93
Baby Boomer Generation	1945	1964	52	71
Generation X	1961	1981	35	55
Generation Y- The Millennials - Gen Next	1975	1995	21	41
Generation Z	1995	2015	0	20

Yes, fax machines are dinosaurs now—even though, shockingly, they are still used in the healthcare industry where I work—but in the 1980s they were hailed as a technological marvel, promising to make our lives easier and free up more time. Subsequently, the introduction of e-mail, the Internet, text messaging, and social media all dazzled with that same promise: making our lives simpler and giving more time for important tasks.

In many ways, technology and its increased speed have demonstrated the power to make our lives simpler and more convenient. For instance, new software called Interface Layer Technology allows itineraries to be created for us with one app that interfaces with our app to make suggestions for our day based on reading our calendar. It might suggest a gift to buy for our sister's birthday, a reservation for a restaurant for lunch near our last morning appointment, or booking of a car to take us to the airport, all based on reading our calendar.

A benefit of smartphones and tablets is the proliferation of apps that offer a plethora of new resources in entertainment, education, finance, personal health, and so much more. In fact, according to a *New York Times* article, health apps are being used widely by researchers who find many apps a far superior way to collect more accurate health and other data from people participating in research studies.

If that bold promise of computing and communication technology—that our lives would be simplified and easier—comes true, then we should have nothing but leisure time in the years to come because the pace of new technology will increase exponentially in the future. The power needed to perform a task will fall by half every 1.5 years. As a result, even smaller and less power-soaking devices will likely proliferate.[77] But we now know from experience that, rather than giving us more leisure time, technology has meant that more demands are placed on us, and stressors increase.

While you cannot argue that technology offers many benefits and the speed of technology will continue to increase, a Google search of the use of the word "joy" shows a steady reduction from 1800 to 2015, and it reached its low point in the 1990s.[78]

The Decline of Use of
the Word "Joy" 1800 - 2015

What a paradox! Computing and communication technology rapidly increase while joy, or at least the use of the word "joy," falls. While I did not particularly like statistics class in college or business school, I learned enough to know that taking two seemingly random variables, like "computing speed" and "the use of the word 'joy,'" and plotting them against each other over time does not necessarily demonstrate statistical correlation and certainly not cause and effect.

Having said that, however, I can speak to my own experience. I am a gadget geek, but I often feel distracted and overwhelmed by the constant digital stimuli in my life. Some people expect a near-instant response to their messages, creating an unhealthy hypervigilance. We can become a slave to the thought that we have to be available almost 24/7—like a doctor on call.

When I noticed my anxiety levels rising with each ping or vibration of my smartphone, I decided I had to take action. Out of self-preservation, I developed new methods to change how I use technology so I can focus my energy on pursuits that evoke the emotion of joy and reduce bad stress. I describe later in the book how I manage my calendar to set aside specific times to manage e-mail messaging. I also turn my phone to "Do Not Disturb" mode during times when I need to focus.

When our daughter Kelsey was in middle school, I often found four teen girls sitting on the couch in our living room working their smartphones with furious speed, checking their social media apps and even texting each other. I would ask, "Hey girls, you're all in the same room. Why don't you talk to each other rather than texting?" They'd glance up at me, shrug, and then go right back to looking at their screens.

When I was a teenager, I used to fight with my siblings over the house phone (you know, the one plugged into the wall), because we all loved to talk to friends on the phone, sometimes for long periods of time.

Another curious thing I have noticed is that the usage patterns of our smartphones vary greatly among the members of our family. I have several conference calls a day for my work and prefer to speak with people rather than corresponding through e-mails, so I use a lot of talk minutes. I use text messaging for quick information exchanges and use apps on my phone and the Internet each day but for short periods of time. Kelsey, who is now in college, uses text messages and data but less talk time. My wife Sherry is somewhere in the middle with her phone use. The graph below represents a typical month of usage for the three of us.

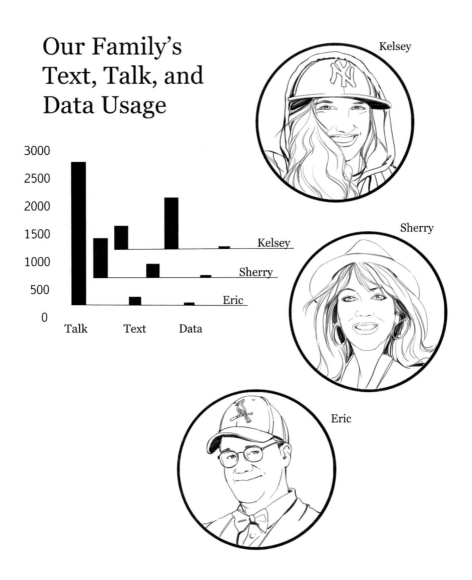

Our Family's Text, Talk, and Data Usage

Kelsey

Sherry

Eric

Because we can do so much on our smartphones and other devices, they have become like an appendage. I see them in back pockets if not in someone's hands or on the table next to our food while we eat. We live in a hyperconnected world.

Just the other day, my wife, Sherry, was expecting a phone call from her cousin Mandy Cook, who was actually calling to talk to me about designing the cover of the book but did not have my number at the time.

Sherry needed to run errands and left her phone with me so that I could talk to Mandy when she called. I did connect with Mandy, an amazing artist who did end up designing the cover of this book. The next day Sherry said that it was so strange to be out and about without her phone, because several times she wanted to look up information, call her sister about something, check directions, and so on, and kept realizing that she was without her primary information and communication tool.

This conversation gave me an idea. What if we took phone sabbaticals every now and then where we leave our phone with a spouse, significant other, or friend in the case of an emergency and spend a whole day without the phone or other digital device?

While these devices are amazing, many people are addicted to them and use them so much that they literally walk by the beauty of creation all around them without noticing, not stopping to smell the roses. They miss the opportunity for conversation and connection with people in a non-digital way. The art of relationship building requires listening with eye contact and empathy. The average American spends more than five hours per day using digital devices on computers and mobile devices, and another four and a half hours watching television. The average person checks his or her mobile phone 150 times a day.

Reading body language and studying the way people behave and interact with others is critical in business and personal relationships, but the younger generation shows a serious decline in making eye contact. Numerous studies have documented that people feel less engaged and emotionally disconnected the less eye contact is made during a conversation. Eye contact communicates caring and helps build empathy.

While smartphones can enhance relationships and offer an opportunity for efficiency, they also distract our minds and take away our focus. So **STOP** looking at your smartphone. I cannot tell you how many times Sherry and I have gone out for dinner and seen couples seated across from each other who never looked up from their phones the entire meal. One of the saddest sights to me are parents with young children who are ignored throughout the meal while Dad watches a game on his phone and Mom posts and chats on Facebook. There is a time for your smartphone and a time to turn it off.

An overreliance on social media also puts a crimp on your time together with friends and family. Spending your free time surfing Facebook, Instagram, Pinterest, or Twitter when you could be with your partner is a missed opportunity. Your gadget is not going to provide happiness and fond memories.

I like a ritual that a colleague of mine, Frazer Buntin, uses. Before he walks in his house after a busy day of work, he turns off his smartphone and puts it in a drawer. He reserves his evening time for his wife and two young daughters. They dine together, get caught up on the activities of the day, do homework, watch some TV, and read stories at bedtime. Sometimes he picks up his phone after his kids are in bed and gets caught up. He believes that the act of physically turning off the phone and putting it in a drawer eliminates the temptation to use it when what he really desires is to devote that time to his family.

I admit that I often overuse my phone. I have adopted another ritual that a friend suggested to enhance relationships and tame the smartphone. When having dinner with friends, he asks everyone to take out their phones and stack them on top of one another with the ringers off in the middle of the table. The first person to pick up their phone during dinner picks up the bill. It is good for a laugh, but also a great way to express, *"Let's take this time to enjoy each other and the food and not be connected to the rest of the world."*

At an executive retreat with colleagues last year I was asked to lead an exercise on the Corporate Performance Athlete initiative at our company. We had about twenty-five people in a large room, and I asked each person to take out their phones, turn their ringers on and their volume all the way up, and then to come and stack their phones on the table in the middle. We made a tower of smartphones that were a cacophony of beeping, ringing, and pinging. I led the group in a meditation exercise with deep breathing and visualization. The group could not stay focused on the meditation because of the stack of smartphones constantly buzzing. That was the point of the exercise. If we want to focus, want to relax, want to meditate, we have to **STOP** looking at our smartphones.

Questions for Reflection

- Do you put away your smartphone in meetings or when you need to be in concentration mode?
- Do you ever turn your phone off or put it away?
- What apps enhance your life and which ones are mostly a waste of time?

CHAPTER 11

STOP Multitasking

We all do it: Texting while walking, sending emails during meetings, chatting on the phone while cooking dinner. In today's society, doing just one thing at a time seems downright luxurious, even wasteful.
  —*Amanda MacMillan,* 12 Reasons to Stop Multitasking Now!

I had the opportunity to visit the Kaiser Innovation Center in Oakland, California, to learn how Kaiser Permanente, one of the largest integrated health systems in the United States, improves the quality of the care delivered to patients. The center is located in an old warehouse and is fascinating because Kaiser builds mock operating rooms and patient rooms and tests several environments to find the ones that contribute most to quality and safety.

One of the greatest innovations discovered at the center, our guide explained to us on our tour, was amazingly simple. Nurses who administered drugs to patients in hospital rooms made far too many errors, which resulted in adverse outcomes. After studying the problem over several weeks, they discovered that the No. 1 factor contributing to errors in drugs administered by nurses to patients in the hospital was distracted nurses. That's right—distracted nurses.

The fix was simple. When it came time for a nurse to administer drugs, the nurse put a brightly colored sash around his/her neck, and all other staff were instructed to not talk to the nurse who was wearing the sash. Also, a circle was painted on the floor around the med cart, and no one was allowed to distract a nurse preparing drugs inside the circle. This sash, like that worn by a contestant in a beauty pageant, and some bright paint cost less than ten dollars and reduced the cost of drug errors by millions of dollars, and, more importantly, saved many lives.

We all multitask at times. Some people claim to be great multitaskers and take great pride in their ability to balance many things at once. I have known people who feel guilty if they are only doing one thing at a time, like listening on a conference call without keeping up with e-mails and text messages simultaneously. Writer Daniel Leviton on theguardian.com describes the pressure to multitask:

> "Our smartphones have become Swiss Army Knife-like appliances that include a dictionary, calculator, web browser, email, Game Boy, appointment calendar, voice recorder, guitar tuner, weather forecaster, GPS, texter, tweeter, Facebook updater, and flashlight. They're more powerful and do more things than the most advanced computer at IBM corporate headquarters 30 years ago. And we use them all the time, part of a 21st-century mania for cramming everything we do into every single spare moment of downtime. We text while we're walking across the street, catch up on email while standing in a queue—and while having lunch with friends, we surreptitiously check to see what our other friends are doing. At the kitchen counter, cozy and secure in our domicile, we write our shopping lists on smartphones while we are listening to that wonderfully informative podcast on urban beekeeping."[79]

Used with Permission by Wiley Publishers New York.

"SWISS ARMY" PHONE

The reality is, however, that our brains were not built for multitasking. That's a widespread myth that contributes to our constant feeling of being on overload. According to MIT neuroscientist Earl Miller, one of the top researchers on divided attention, "Our brains are not wired to multitask well . . . when people think they're multitasking, they're actually just switching from one task to another very rapidly. And every time they do, there's a cognitive cost."[80] So to get the most joy out of your life and ease that guilt that you cannot juggle a half dozen balls at once, you can relax and **STOP** multitasking.

When we constantly switch between tasks, we train our brains into developing bad habits. When we complete a small task, such as responding to an e-mail, we feel a tiny sense of accomplishment. Our brains release a little bit of dopamine, our reward hormone. We like this instant gratification, and so we develop a habit each time we give in to the craving for more dopamine. We get the illusion that we are accomplishing more than we are, because we are checking things off our mental list. In addition, studies show that children who multitask while using electronic devices showed lower self-esteem and social skills.[81]

The problem is that multitasking actually lowers our work quality and efficiency. It becomes more difficult to organize thoughts and filter out irrelevant information because we are not focusing. A University of London study demonstrated that subjects who multitasked while performing cognitive tasks experienced significant drops in their IQs. In fact, the IQ declines were similar to what you see in individuals who skip a night of sleep or who smoke marijuana.[82] So dopamine addiction is the equivalent of an addiction to dope.

How do we stop multitasking? First, try to use the rule of two—do not perform more than two tasks at a time and preferably just one. A French study found the human brain can handle two complicated tasks without too much trouble because it has two lobes that can divide responsibility equally between the two. Add a third task, however, and it can overwhelm the frontal cortex and increase the number of mistakes you make.[83]

I hasten to add, however, that driving and looking at your smartphone are not two acceptable tasks to perform together. Ten percent of all fatal automobile accidents are due to distracted driving, whether texting, talking, or looking for directions.[84] If you use your phone for navigation, set it up before you start driving and then leave it alone and just listen. Multitasking can be dangerous and it creates a false sense of accomplishment, but there is no substitute for monotasking because it offers the highest level of focus and concentration.

Second, put away the things that distract you. If your Swiss-Army-knife smartphone is too tempting to have on your desk during a meeting, put it away or, better yet, turn it completely off. If the TV in the background keeps you from listening to your spouse, either pause it while you talk or turn it off. One study from the University of Essex found that just having a cell phone nearby during personal conversations—even if neither of you is using it—can cause friction and trust issues.[85]

Third, practice O.H.I.O.—only **h**andle **i**t **o**nce. Efficiency experts recommended this simple practice to increase effectiveness for many years. If you only handle an incoming item one time, then the task is completed quicker, and you can move on to something else. For instance, if you open an e-mail, rather than scanning it quickly only to leave it in your inbox with the thought of revisiting it later, you will handle it more than once. Rather, open it and quickly determine if it is important. If so, read it and either respond, file, forward, or delete. Done. I like to keep a clean inbox and only leave items in my inbox that I have not yet read or addressed.

The science of multitasking is fascinating. There are many interesting studies that generally conclude that we function at a much higher level by not multitasking. In fact, our lives may hang in the balance if we haven't yet decided to **STOP** multitasking. We know the dangers of texting while driving and not paying attention while we walk down the street. Studies with rats show that if pushing a lever releases dopamine into their brain, they like it so much that they will push the lever until they overdose and die. We know the dangers of drug addiction but addiction to anything, including multitasking, can be just as dangerous,

---

Questions for Reflection

- How often do you multitask?
- What are examples of tasks you do when multitasking?
- Can you think of a funny or tragic story about someone multitasking?

CHAPTER 12

STOP Talking Too Much

People don't care how much you know until they know how much you care.
—Theodore Roosevelt

Listening is a skill and an art. It is hard work and takes discipline. A good listener monitors and mirrors to some extent the body language of the person talking. A good listener clarifies or repeats back what is said to make sure he or she understands. If you are forming your next comment in your mind, getting ready to get it out the moment the other person stops talking, then you are not listening. If you interrupt, you are not listening. Most of all, it is difficult to listen if you're talking. So just **STOP** talking too much.

Have you ever been in a situation where people talk over each other, constantly interrupting to get in their point? It reminds me of the presidential debates in 2016 where you could hardly hear what the candidates were saying for all the talk-overs and interruptions. By truly listening to another person, you build trust and develop empathy. If you talk too much, the other person may feel like you really don't care what he or she thinks. You send the message that you only care about expressing your opinions, your knowledge, and your information that you want to impart. There's a reason God gave us two ears and one mouth: we should listen twice as much as we talk.

In my first career job after graduating from college, I was trained in insurance sales by one of the finest sales organizations in the country,

Northwestern Mutual Life. While I haven't sold insurance for years, I have continued to put into practice some of the key lessons I learned from the extensive sales training I received.

First, we learned listening skills and practiced them in the training room. We put this into practice when meeting with prospective clients in what we called an interview, because we asked several guided questions about our prospect's goals, finances, resources, insurance coverage, and the like. At no time during the interview were we to "sell" our company, our products, or ourselves. The focus was squarely on the other person.

Of course, when agreeing to meet with an insurance salesperson, a prospect naturally has defenses up and often up high. The prospect expects to be sold. At the end of the interview, however, I would say something like, "Thank you for meeting with me today and sharing this information. I would like to have some time to think about it and get back together soon to share some ideas. Is that okay?" Rarely did I receive a flat "no."

At the second interview, the conversation began with my asking more questions to clarify the information. Only when I'd gone through this process did I share a proposal, tailored to the needs of each person, family, or business.

The best salespeople are the best listeners because they set out to match a product or solution to a specific need or desire. I learned that as a twenty-two-year-old kid right out of college and have found that it works in just about every situation. Some of the best meetings involve few words spoken by me other than questions that open a dialogue. I cringe when I observe colleagues walk into a meeting with a client and proceed to dominate the conversation.

You know you might be talking too much once you open your eyes and look for cues. Like a game of tennis, if someone decides to hog the ball instead of volleying, the game will not be much fun. People generally let us know when we are hogging the ball. Their eyes wander, they get fidgety and appear distracted. They will respond with polite smiles and nods, while they look for the closest exit. These are cues that you need to stop talking and serve the ball to them.

A helpful tip: control your talking by responding to a question with a single thoughtful sentence. Composing your response carefully before speaking is harder than a come-to-mind, come-to-mouth response. If people are interested in what you have to say, they will prompt you for more information. Mark Twain said: "I sat down to write you a short letter, but I did not have enough time so I wrote you a long one instead." The point is clear: it is easier to talk too much than to think about the most appropriate words to say.

Being a good listener is not just about being less annoying or showing someone you care, it is essential in understanding another human being. One of my favorite professors in the MBA program at the University of Chicago Booth School of Business was Nick Epley, professor of behavioral science. In his book *Mindwise: Why We Misunderstand What Others Think, Believe, Feel, and Want,* he describes that to truly read someone's mind, not in a mystical sense of the term, but to really understand what and how someone thinks, we need to work very hard at *perspective taking*, putting ourselves inside of their mind. He suggests asking questions like, "Would I like this movie if I were a woman? If I were my wife, what would I want for my birthday? How would I feel if I were living in poverty? Would I understand this presentation if I were one of our clients?"[86]

Really understanding where a person is coming from goes beyond *perspective taking* to *perspective getting*, as Epley describes. Asking someone what he or she thinks directly, or surveying a group of people, will help to get perspective. For instance, I could ask Sherry what she wants for her birthday. Her first response will be something like, "Oh, nothing," but follow-up questions like, "What have you been wanting for a long time but did not want to spend the money on?" might help get perspective.

When Abraham Lincoln was asked to offer a few appropriate remarks at the dedication of the military cemetery at Gettysburg, Pennsylvania, he was not the keynote speaker. Edward Everett, the Massachusetts statesman, was the lead speaker and spoke for two hours before Lincoln came to the podium to deliver the Gettysburg Address. The talk was so brief, two hundred words, that he was finished before the photographer could take a quality photo. And yet, we love to visit the Lincoln Memorial in Washington, DC, and read those famous words carved in granite. Relatively few people even know Edward Everett's name. Lincoln said that day: "The world will little note, nor long remember what we say here . . ." Quite wrong, we do long remember Lincoln's profound few words, but Everett talked so much that no one remembers. Lincoln knew, more than most, when to **STOP** talking.

Questions for Reflection

- Do you know anyone who talks too much?
- In what situations, if any, do you talk too much?
- What one behavior would help you gain or get perspective from another person?

CHAPTER 13

STOP Overloading Your Schedule

It is not enough to be busy. So are the ants. The question is: What are we busy about?

—Henry David Thoreau

Are you so busy that you don't know if you're coming or going? If I did not actively and consciously manage my schedule, it would fill up to the point that it would manage me. I came to the realization about a year ago that one of the largest sources of stress in my life was lack of control over my time, particularly my work time. The solution for me was to **STOP** overloading my calendar.

Richard Swenson, MD, coined the term "margin" in his book of the same title to describe the need we all have for space in our lives. Look at the page you are reading now; it has a margin at the top and bottom and on the sides. It has space between paragraphs. What if the type on this page were pushed all the way out to the edges with no space between paragraphs? It would be so dense that it would be difficult to read and would likely increase your blood pressure while trying. That is the point of margin. We need room to breathe.

Here is an example from the book *Margin*. "Marginless is being thirty minutes late to the doctor's office, because you were twenty minutes late getting out of the hairdresser's, because you were ten minutes late dropping the children off at school, because the car ran out of gas two blocks from the gas station—and you forgot your purse."[87]

We have all had marginless days, but is this type of day the exception or the rule in your life? Do you have enough margin?

The key tactic to the Corporate Performance Athlete initiative at my company, Evolent Health, is management of our calendars. The overriding principle of calendar management is that you are in control of your calendar. In his book *Shine*, Edward Hallowell, MD, describes the relationship between brain science and peak performance. He writes, "Smart people underperform when their circuits get overloaded."[88]

When you consider your schedule, you may not feel like you have much control, but you have a choice about how to spend most of the hours in your day. The most powerful word in the English language is "no." Determining how to spend your time, deciding what meetings and calls to accept, and creating white space on your calendar are critical factors to reducing stress and freeing up energy to focus on your top priorities.

Kristi Ling, happiness strategist, offers three tips to manage our calendars:

1. Make it a positive habit to give yourself a chance to think mindfully about obligations and projects before saying "Yes" to them. **If your soul isn't telling you, "Heck yeah!" then seriously consider a "No."**

2. Even if you're making an effort to only allow things that feed your soul (or things that are absolutely necessary) on your schedule, sometimes your schedule will still become too full. Make a point each week or month to check in with your calendar and ask yourself, "**Is my schedule too full to live fully?**" If the answer is *yes*, look for some things to drop, or reschedule for a time when your load is lighter.

3. **Schedule unscheduled time.** Purposely leave some mornings, afternoons, and even entire days blank, so you can have some time now and then to just zone out or do something you feel inspired by in those moments. I block out time in my schedule to have absolutely nothing planned. When I do, I always end

up thanking myself. Some of the best times I've ever had are the spontaneous ones—when you just go where the wind takes you.[89]

In my experience, if I do not add time to my calendar for things like exercise, writing, planning, thinking, personal events, and other priorities, they tend to slip off my radar screen. I use a digital calendar that syncs with my laptop and smartphone, but sometimes I need to print it out on 11x17-inch paper so that I can see it more clearly and make notes. Also, I color-code my calendar to differentiate between personal events, conference calls, travel times, planning times, and the like. Here is my list of color-coded categories:

I set aside three thirty-minute time slots three times each business day to check and respond to e-mail messages. These scheduled times allow me to stop checking them constantly. I am getting to the place where I do not look at my phone or laptop during conference calls and meetings, which allows me to focus on the topic at hand.

Having said that, many meetings are triple-yawners and involve far too many people. I try to get out of those meetings by asking the organizer for the agenda in advance and whether it is critical that I attend. Finally, I suggest using the rule of three with respect to e-mail volleys. If an e-mail conversation has reached round three, it is time to pick up the phone or walk over to the person's office on the string and talk.

Another ritual for me is to schedule ramp-up and ramp-down times at the beginning and end of each week. During my ramp-down time on Friday afternoons, I review my calendar for the following two weeks with an eye toward declining the triple-yawners or reassigning meetings and calls that do not require my participation. This step ensures that my highest priorities are scheduled first.

My ramp-up time on my calendar at the beginning of each week helps me get in the right frame of mind for the workweek and my ramp-down time helps me leave the week behind. I feel like I finished the week well and made plans for the following week. I also schedule office hours at the end of each day, like a college professor, where I am available to anyone on my team without a scheduled appointment.

I am not suggesting that you adopt my methods or that my methods are the best practice. Please use any tool that works for you, whether a paper calendar, digital, or otherwise. I tend to be hyperorganized, because my memory is bad, and I need more structure than most. When I put it all together it looks like my calendar is jam-packed, even overloaded.

Make no mistake, I am very busy, but if you look closely, you can see that I have blocked out time on my calendar to work out, time to write (one of my favorite activities), time to prepare, travel time, and other "non-meeting" events, because I schedule "meetings" with myself. Here is a screenshot from my calendar last week at the time of this writing.

A Week from My Calendar

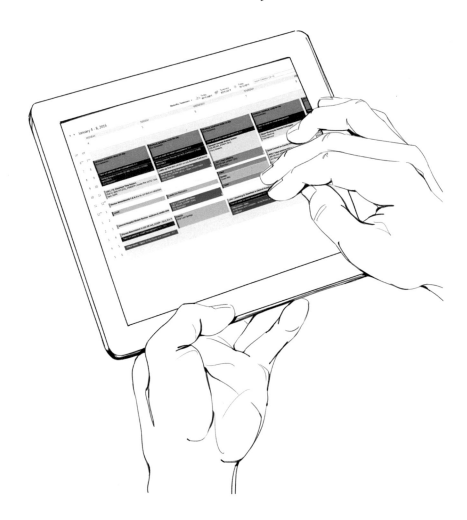

Another benefit of managing your schedule from the perspective of the Corporate Performance Athlete is that you work less overtime. For some folks, overtime represents a workweek of more than forty hours. For me, fifty hours of work each week is average. I love to work, so that fits my personality and the demands of my career just fine. Occasionally I will work more than fifty hours, but when I find that necessary, building in the necessary blocks for planning and preparation and managing around my top priorities relieves a great deal of stress. In fact, if I have made significant progress on my top priorities for the week, I can end the workweek with no regrets for not accomplishing everything on my list and do not feel the need to work overtime to check off a few more tasks.

One of the greatest benefits for me in managing my calendar according to priorities is that I trust my colleagues. Delegating work to people provides them with an opportunity to step up and stretch into areas that help them grow. In the healthcare industry where I work, we have a common goal of people working at the "top of their license." This means that a doctor should focus her time on the highest-end skills based on her education, training, and credentials, and a nurse practitioner, physician's assistant, and nurse all need to do the same. This requires delegation of work to people who are educated and trained to handle that task. For instance, if you hire a lawyer, you don't want to pay the hourly rate of the partner in the law firm to do basic research that a law clerk can perform at a fraction of the hourly rate. To delegate work, you need the right team of trusted colleagues or teammates or friends.

Jim Collins, in his classic business book *Good to Great*, sums it up well by saying "leaders of companies that go from good to great start not with 'where' but with 'who.' They start by getting the right people on the bus, the wrong people off the bus, and the right people in the right seats."[90] If you surround yourself with great people, you can truly **STOP** overloading your calendar and create an environment where everyone thrives.

Questions for Reflection

- How much margin do you have in your life?
- Do you block out preparation times and other uninterruptible times on your calendar?
- What other steps can you take to create more margin?

CHAPTER 14

STOP Worrying

Therefore do not worry about tomorrow, for tomorrow will worry about itself.
Each day has enough trouble of its own.

—*Jesus, Matthew 6:34* (NIV)

I come from a long line of worriers. My mother worries for each member of the family as her mother did before her and so on. This womanly worry is rooted in love and concern for the welfare of their families. It is sweet to know that someone cares enough to worry. At least one of my sisters has picked up this fine tradition. I refer to my mother as the "designated worrier," because she worries enough for all of us and we don't need more than one worrier.

Some of the men in my family, however, probably should worry more. We are perhaps too oblivious to reality to take it seriously and had we worried a bit more, perhaps we would have made fewer mistakes. But the fact remains that while a little bit of worry is helpful, as an early indicator of the fight-or-flight response to danger, too much worry can be debilitating.

Worry is focusing on what might go wrong. You know you are worrying when you are plagued by uneasy thoughts and over-concern about all the possible scenarios that could arise from a circumstance or problem. Some insist that worrying can help prevent something bad from happening. However, in reality, worry is a form of anxiety, and excessive anxiety can be a serious mental health issue with physical implications. Lack of sleep and restless sleep, headaches, ulcers, and other serious stress-related physical problems all result from too much worry. Worry affects everyday life so much that it interferes with appetite, digestion, sleep, and relationships.

Many famous people have commented on the topic of worry. Here are some of their quotes starting with my favorite perspective on the topic from Jesus.

> *"Therefore do not worry about tomorrow, for tomorrow will worry about itself. Each day has enough trouble of its own."*
>
> *—Jesus, Matthew 6:34*

> *"Do not worry about your difficulties in mathematics. I can assure you mine are still greater."*
>
> *—Albert Einstein*

> *"Life is too short to worry about anything. You had better enjoy it because the next day promises nothing."*
>
> *—Eric Davis*

> *"Thomas Jefferson once said, 'We should never judge a president by his age, only by his works.' And ever since he told me that, I stopped worrying."*
>
> *—Ronald Reagan*

> *"My life has been filled with terrible misfortune; most of which never happened."*
>
> *—Michel de Montaigne*

Has anyone ever suggested to you that you worry too much? I ask this question because if you are a worrier, you may not recognize it unless others have brought it to your attention. There is good news for you: 85 percent of what we worry about never happens, according to a study. Of the 15 percent that did happen, 79 percent of subjects discovered either they could handle the difficulty better than expected, or the difficulty taught them a lesson worth learning. That means that 97 percent of what you worry over is not much more than a fearful mind punishing you with exaggerations and misperceptions.[91]

Many of the suggestions in this book are good remedies for worry—mindful meditation, thoughtfulness about eating and drinking, physical exercise, rest, et al. Another tip is to designate time to worry. Take fifteen minutes of dedicated time and write down everything you are worried about and take another fifteen minutes reflecting, meditating, and letting go. A friend of mine calls it his "What's Bugging Kevin?" list. Once he gets it down on paper, he's not fretting over that mental list.

The key is to let go of the things you can't control, which is most things, and developing an action plan for those you can control. Worry is a form of mistrust. It is a glass-half-empty perspective like Murphy's Law: Whatever can go wrong, will go wrong. Take some time to study positive psychology, like the work of Martin Seligman, which is a specific field of study and not the same as pop psychology or feel-good positive mental attitude (PMA) books and conferences. PMA motivation has its place, like taking a bath or shower. Both are important but they don't last. Rewiring negative thought patterns, which is what positive psychology espouses, can lead to a lasting reduction in worry.

Learn new habits, learn new methods to redirect or dismiss worry. As you learn new methods for managing worry, slow down and redirect and remind yourself to **STOP** worrying.

Questions for Reflection

1. Have you ever worried about a situation that either did not happen or turned out much better than expected?
2. Has more than one person suggested to you that you worry too much?
3. Have you ever experienced physical effects related to worry? If so, what?

Holding Back Your Life

CHAPTER 15

STOP Spending Impulsively

. . . Our impulses are too strong for our judgment sometimes.
— *Thomas Hardy,* Tess of the D'Urbervilles

To me, impulsive means foolish. But if a person's not a little impulsive, they don't have a pulse.
—*Jarod Kintz,* Whenever You're Gone, I'm Here for You

I write this next section, entitled "**STOP** Holding Back Your Life," and this chapter on impulsive spending, as an expert. I have wasted a lot of money in my life and much of it can be attributed to impulsive spending and other stupid decisions. Fortunately, I am learning from my mistakes. I am glad to pass along my perspectives from lessons learned the hard way and some good book-learning as well.

Impulse spending is just what it sounds like: buying goods and services on impulse because they caught your attention or seemed like a great deal in the moment. It's not a preplanned purchase. Impulse spending is driven by emotion because it temporarily makes you feel better. Impulse spending is another activity that provides an immediate reward and triggers chemicals in the brain that make you feel good.

According to a study by CreditCards.com, three out of four adults in the United States make impulse purchases.[92] Nearly one in three of the impulse buyers in this survey said they had spent $500 or more on such a purchase; 10 percent spent $1,000 or more. Respondents said they typically buy impulsively when they are excited, bored, or sad. The survey showed gender also plays a role.

"We found that men and women impulse shop about the same amount, but the way they feel and how much they spend when they do it are different," said CreditCards.com senior analyst Matt Schulz.

- Men were significantly more likely than women to spend serious money on that unplanned purchase. While just 7 percent of the women said they had spent $500 or more, 21 percent of the men did. Men also made more impulse purchases of $1,000 or more.
- Women tend to keep their impulse purchases small, under $25.
- Men are more than twice as likely to make an impulse purchase when they're intoxicated.
- Women are twice as likely to buy impulsively when they are sad.
- Women are more likely to regret making an impulse purchase: 52 percent of the women vs. 46 percent of the men said they experienced buyer's remorse at one time or another.

While the location of the purchase doesn't seem to matter—survey respondents said they were as likely to make an impulse purchase online as in person—age and education does seem to make a difference.

- Nearly 90 percent of the millennials said they'd made an impulse purchase, compared to just 56 percent of the seniors.
- College graduates were also more likely to make spur-of-the-moment purchases (86 percent) than non-college graduates (64 percent).[93]

The dollars add up quickly. According to a study by a British utility company, men thoughtlessly spend more than $2,000 per year while women fritter away more than $1,500. As a couple, that is more than $3,500 per year, $35,000 over ten years, and $70,000 over twenty years.[94]

So why do we spend impulsively? The answer, like so many behaviors, could be psychological. According to *Psychology Today*, impulse buying is related to anxiety and unhappiness. Controlling it could help improve your psychological well-being.[95]

Some people possess a personality trait called an "impulse buying tendency," a habit of making impulsive purchases. That might sound innocent, but a number of behaviors go along with this trait that reflect its detrimental influence.

First, impulse buyers are more social, status conscious, and image concerned. The impulse buyer may therefore buy as a way to look good in the eyes of others. Second, impulse buyers tend to experience more anxiety and difficulty controlling their emotions, which may make it harder to resist emotional urges to impulsively spend money. Third, impulse buyers tend to experience less happiness, and so may buy as a way to improve their mood. Lastly, impulse buyers are less likely to consider the consequences of their spending; they just want to have it.[96]

In order to put a **STOP** to impulse spending, develop new methods or heuristics (rules of thumb) to guide your decisions. First, before you make a purchase, ask yourself a simple question: "Did I plan to buy this, or did I get the urge to buy it just now?"

If you didn't plan to buy it, you're probably experiencing an impulse-buying urge. By putting that product back on the shelf and refusing to purchase it, you're doing something to help yourself. You're rejecting the idea that by purchasing that product you'll be happier, better respected, or more complete. In so doing, you'll not only get to keep more of your money, but you'll become a smarter consumer and possibly a happier person.[97]

Second, a heuristic that is helpful is to make a list of things to buy. This list could be your grocery list or a Christmas list or a list of things for your home. Your wish list of things to buy could require you to save, perhaps for a long period of time. For instance, Sherry and I have a shared grocery list that syncs between our devices. When we go to the store, we buy the things on our list. Occasionally we will add a few other items to the grocery cart, but the list keeps us focused.

I have a bucket list that includes the purchase of a 1954 Chevy pickup truck, fully restored. I have wanted this since I was a teenager, and I do plan to buy it someday. However, I will not buy it until I can do so knowing that more important priorities, like college education for our kids, are fully funded.

A third rule of thumb is that once you are able, set aside specific dollars for play money. Then, when you go shopping for fun, you have a specific amount of money that you have decided in advance is okay to spend however you wish. If you see something that you really want and you have enough stashed away in your play money fund, you can purchase it without guilt because it was part of the plan.

Finally, and perhaps most important, do not use a credit card to buy something impulsively unless you have the cash back home to pay it off on the next bill. Credit card debt is out of control for many Americans and much of that debt is due to impulsive spending. Do I expect to never make an impulsive purchase in my life? No. However, awareness of the root causes of impulsive spending and some simple techniques to keep spending under control go a long way for me as I attempt to **STOP** spending impulsively.

Questions for Reflection

- How often do you spend impulsively?
- If you ever spend impulsively, is it for small or big-ticket items?
- Do you make lists of things to buy and save up for big purchases?

CHAPTER 16

STOP Buying Things of Little Value

In the US and much of the industrialized world, cheap clothes are everywhere. At any fast-fashion chain store, you'll find piles upon piles of jeans that cost less than $20. The problem is, all that low-cost clothing is produced, sold, and finally discarded in mass quantities, which has serious consequences for the environment, the workers paid poorly to make them, and even the mental well-being of the people buying them.

—Mark Bain, "The Case for Expensive Clothes," The Atlantic

High quality costs less than poor quality in the long run. We live in a consumer society. With retail stores and online shopping, there is no shortage of products to buy at just about every price point. Buying things with low value is a waste of money, despite the low cost.

Let's start with food. Fresh produce and high-quality healthy foods typically cost more than some of the packaged food in the middle aisles of the grocery store, and a high-quality meal at a restaurant will cost more than fast food. But consider that the poor-quality food you consume will make you less healthy and zap your energy. So the true cost of unhealthy food is much more than the price tag on the box of the processed, sugary, empty-calorie product. The economic toll of poor health alone, not to mention the impact on the environment, is enormous. When friends complain about the cost of organic, healthy food, I tell them that they are going to pay one way or the other. My family and I choose to pay a little extra and invest in our health.

A report from the Worldwatch Institute called *Overfed and Underfed: The Global Epidemic of Malnutrition* documented the real costs of obesity related to poor diet—and this report does NOT include the other effects of poor diet such as heart disease, cancer, diabetes, dementia, autoimmune diseases, and osteoporosis. Here were some of the conclusions of that report:

- Obese people account for a disproportionate share of health-related absences from work.
- Obesity accounts for 7 percent of lost productivity due to sick leave and disability.
- 7 percent of all of North Carolina's healthcare expenditures are related to obesity.
- Obese people visit their physicians 40 percent more than normal weight people.
- Obese people are 2.5 times more likely to require drugs prescribed for cardiovascular and circulation disorders.
- Liposuction is the No. 1 form of cosmetic surgery in the United States, with 400,000 operations a year.
- More than 100,000 people a year have gastric bypass surgery.[98]

According to a recent study in *The New England Journal of Medicine*, we're spending a whopping $20,000 per person for each extra year of life gained from medical interventions like drugs and surgery.[99]

The reality is that the actual cost of high-quality food does not have to be more than food that promotes poor health. Preparing healthy menus for eating well at home and shopping with a specific list of healthy foods will save money over eating out at fast-food restaurants and impulse buys at the grocery store. Buying just enough fresh food for a day or two rather than throwing food away that has been kept for too long will also save money.

Budget expert Clark Howard says that shopping at your local farmers' market can save up to 30 percent or more, and you are helping the environment by buying local.[100] Keep the pantry stocked with only healthy food and snacks rather than large quantities of food laden with chemicals and preservatives that keep forever, and you will save money in the long run. Buying quality not only has health benefits, it does not have to cost more if you plan right.

Employers are experiencing increased healthcare costs and reduced productivity and therefore are investing in cultures of health as a business strategy. If you have a cafeteria at work or school, check out the healthy options, which may now cost less. I work with many leading-edge employers, including hospitals, that now subsidize the cost of healthy foods and increase the cost of unhealthy food in their cafeterias so that the healthy food is a bargain. Some employers are changing vending machines as well, where you will spend less for bottled water than for soda. Some employers ask their vending machine suppliers to turn the products backwards with the nutritional labels facing the front so that buyers can compare nutritional content.

Of course, purchasing quality makes sense in every spending category. Take clothing, for example. I have made the mistake before of buying cheap dress shoes and suits only to see them crack or split. Within two years, I wind up throwing them in the trash can. Spending the extra money on a high-quality pair of men's dress shoes and a tailored suit made of fine fabric has numerous benefits. First, they look great. Second, they are more comfortable. Third, they last longer, and the shoes can be refurbished when needed. A high-quality men's suit comes with two pairs of slacks to extend the useful life because we put more wear and tear in the pants than the jacket.

Consider the following math:

Cost of Men's Shoes and Suits over Time

	Low-quality Shoes	High-quality Shoes	Low-quality Suit	High-quality Suit
Purchase Price	$75	$300	$300	$1000
Years of Use	2	15	2	10
Average Cost per Year	$37.50	$20	$150	$100
Look and Feel	Not so great	Great	Not so great	Great

Would you rather look and feel great for $120 per year, or look and feel shabby at a cost of $187.50?

Planning ahead for clothing purchases, auto purchases, home purchases, or just about anything makes perfect sense. Many fine men's stores have semiannual or annual sales. Watch for those.

Also, for durable goods and some clothing, consider used rather than new. Buying a high-quality, low-mileage used vehicle generally makes sense over buying a new one off the lot, only to watch the value drop by 30 percent or more as soon as you drive out of the dealership. My favorite men's store in Nashville is a high-quality consignment store. It offers only the best quality brands and some new clothes and accessories as well. I have purchased some great clothes for much less than retail cost new.

My wife Sherry is an expert at finding bargains. She knows exactly what consignment and thrift stores to shop at and what days are the best when new shipments arrive. Our home looks great and she looks fabulous, even though some of the items were purchased at a low cost. She has a lot of fun shopping, too.

We have found that if we **STOP** buying things of little value, the quality of our lives improves, we have the thrill of getting a great deal, and we save money in the long run.

Questions for Reflection

- What percentage of your food purchases are high value?
- How do you buy clothes?
- What examples can you think of where you made a low-value purchase?

CHAPTER 17

STOP the Debt

I am positive that personal finance is 80 percent behavior and only 20 percent head knowledge. Our concentration on behavior—realizing that most folks have a good idea of what to do with money but not how to do it—has led us to a different view of personal finance.

—Dave Ramsey, The Total Money Makeover

Dave Ramsey, nationally syndicated radio talk-show host and best-selling author, stands out as my favorite author on the topic of managing money. Central to his philosophy is the critical importance of getting out of debt. Debt is mostly about behavior—bad behavior—and with debt comes much worry and stress. Debt stress robs us of joy.

I had the opportunity to meet Dave and his wife Sharon a few years ago at their beautiful home in middle Tennessee and really appreciated their humility and generous spirit. They are clearly living a joyous life, one that is enhanced by the principles he teaches, including not having debt. My brother Todd has taught Ramsey's Financial Peace University courses for several years, and I have witnessed the transformation that it has made in his life and in the lives of others.

Money is a leading source of stress for Americans. According to a survey by the American Psychological Association, 73 percent of the respondents claimed that money was a significant source of stress in their lives.[101] Today, more than three out of every four American families are in debt, according to the Federal Reserve's Survey of Consumer Finances.[102]

The majority of people struggle with money problems. People lose jobs, or experience an unexpected health crisis, lawsuit, divorce, or death of a provider who has not adequately planned for the future. In fact, the cost of healthcare is so high that 41 percent of adults (ages 19–64) reported that they had medical debt or trouble paying medical bills, according to *The Commonwealth Fund Health Insurance Survey*.[103] Of course, many financial problems are self-inflicted. Either way, these issues lead to tremendous stress.

Some people live in denial and just ignore their financial problems. Of course, they only get worse until they lead to repossession of property and bankruptcy. Others are so aware of the financial problems that they lose sleep, overeat, stop exercising, and abuse substances. As matters get worse, depression and anger set in, and relationships begin to unravel. I do not paint a nice picture, but the debilitating effects of financial problems are often either the result of debt or exacerbated by debt.

There have been two times in my life where I was in a staggering amount of debt. The first time was in my late twenties and early thirties where I was in a sales career on straight commission income. The problem was not the income. It was my impulsive spending. I tried to impress people with the trappings of success. In fact, I was taught a philosophy from an early boss to "Fake it 'til you make it." This idea was based on the mistaken notion that people want to do business with successful people, and if you look and act successful, you will have more success. That's a pile of malarkey!

Fortunately, I left that company and boss and found a home with a new company and boss who helped me create a structure of living on a fixed income and strict budget and apply all excess income to debt reduction. Three years later, the excess debt was gone. The second time was more recently, in my early fifties, when a messy divorce and legal fees resulted in a large amount of debt.

My new, wonderful wife and I downsized and worked on a plan to drastically reduce our debt. We are not totally out of debt yet but making good progress and enjoying the freedom of living a simpler, less cluttered, and orderly life. The amount of stress that these times produced in my life, and for my family, took a heavy toll. During both of those times in my life, I formed some unhealthy habits as a result. However, as a result of stopping many of the behaviors discussed in this book, including massive debt reduction, I've experienced enhanced well-being, joy, and productivity. Every bad behavior I've ditched has been worth the sacrifice or temporary discomfort. I strive each day to walk my talk.

Bankruptcy is unfortunately the outcome for many who have let debt get so far out of control that they face a judge. It is not short or sweet like the chapter of this book. My intent here is not to give you a debt-reduction plan—Dave Ramsey has already done that—but to encourage you to **STOP** the debt and build a plan to get out as soon as possible.

Questions for Reflection

- If you have debt, do you have a debt-reduction plan?
- If you have debt, how would your life be different if it were gone?
- What have you purchased with debt that you wish you hadn't, if anything?

CHAPTER 18

STOP Spending Time with People Who Bring You Down

Associate with men of good quality if you esteem your own reputation; for it is far better to be alone than to be in bad company.

—*George Washington*

If you want to soar with the eagles, don't hang out with the turkeys.

—*Author Unknown*

You are the company that you keep. Do you have any negative people in your life? When you spend time with those people, do you feel lighter or heavier afterward?

We all know difficult and negative people. In many cases, you cannot avoid them, especially if they are a family member or a coworker. While it may be impossible to avoid these folks completely, and some of them may be close family members who you love dearly, creating boundaries and limiting your exposure is critically important so that they do not drain your energy or, worse, rub off on you.

I have experienced some colleagues and clients who were so negative that I felt like packing my bags and running for the hills. One client was so negative that everyone I knew who ever met her had the same reaction: *Get me out of here.* I tried hard to have a positive dialogue with her, to listen to her concerns, some of which were valid, only to realize that this relationship was a one-way street and was not going anywhere nice. The ironic thing is that this woman worked for the same company for thirty years and retired.

My colleagues and I were baffled by how someone that negative could last that long without being fired. She would dominate every meeting without any regard for who she might offend. She would explain at great length every problem and yet offered no ideas about how to solve the problem and promptly shot down anything that anyone shared to address it. She was intelligent and experienced and many of her observations were reasonable, but they were so buried in the morass of criticism, judgment, and complaints that even her good points were obscured.

In organizations, I've often seen an unwillingness to root out a person who brings everybody else down. Corporate leaders often underestimate the havoc that a difficult personality can wreak. A single toxic person can have a devastating effect on the workplace, according to several studies. That "hurricane employee" can cause a 30 to 40 percent drop in a team's overall performance, according to a Rotterdam School of Management study by Will Felps, Terence R. Mitchell, and Eliza Byington.[104]

Even worse, when you hire a single toxic individual, your most valued employees are 54 percent more likely to quit, according to Cornerstone OnDemand, which looked at data from 63,000 hires—only 3 to 5 percent of whom were ultimately fired for toxic behavior.[105] Shockingly, that 54 percent number held true even if there was only one bad apple for every 20 good employees. That toxic employee costs an average of $12,800 in additional hiring costs to replace the good employees who quit. Multiply that one number across the board, along with the cost to the emotional culture, and you start to get the picture.

There are different types of negative people, such as:

- **The Know-It-All**—Like the Mac Davis song says, "It's Hard to be Humble." This know-it-all thinks he or she is great and always right. The know-it-all has an opinion on every topic and seems to know more than anyone else. This unpleasant personality often fails to be dissuaded by facts to the contrary.

- **Poor, Poor, Pitiful Me**—Like the Linda Ronstadt song, this personality often feels sorry for himself or herself. The person complains about never doing anything right and never being good enough. This person suffers from the victim complex.

- **The Rebel**—Like the character John Bender played by Judd Nelson in the classic teen movie from the 1980s, *The Breakfast Club*, this person draws attention by going against the grain and takes pride in being the contrarian to the point of being obnoxious.

- **The Sarcastic One**—This character reminds me of Dr. Perry Cox on *Scrubs,* played by John McGinley, who expressed through frequent and sometimes incredibly long rants during which he viciously verbally attacked almost every character on the show.

No matter the form of the negative personality—and I list only a few types above—these toxic people often exaggerate and say things simply to get a rise out of their audience. My first suggestion: do not go there. Arguing with a negative person will generally not change Negative Ned's mind, and this exercise will only leave you frustrated. My second suggestion is that if you must be around a negative person, try to make sure you are in groups with other positive people. If nothing else, at least you have a shared experience with others and perhaps the group will soften or even neutralize the tone of the conversation. Don't get your hopes up too high on this point.

Steering conversations to lighter topics may also help. Negative people often have strong, sometimes controversial opinions on just about every topic imaginable. While we are all entitled to our opinions, we don't have to throw gasoline on a fire. Do your best to keep the conversation light.

The best tip: avoid these negative people, and, if possible, drop them from your life. I like the advice that Seth Godin provided in his May 12, 2016, blog called *The Toddler Strategy:*

> Most people don't get too upset at anything a two-year-old kid says to them.
>
> That's because we don't believe that toddlers have a particularly good grasp on the nuances of the world, nor do they possess much in the way of empathy. Mostly, though, it turns out that getting mad at a toddler doesn't do any good, because he's not going to change as a result (not for a few years, anyway).
>
> Couldn't the same be said for your uninformed critics? For the people who bring you down without knowing any better, for those that sabotage your best work, or undermine your confidence for selfish reasons?
>
> It's hardly productive to ruin your day and your work trying to teach these folks a lesson.
>
> Better, I think, to treat them like a toddler. Buy them a lollipop, smile and walk away.
>
> —*Seth Godin blog (used with permission)*

Another tip for managing negative people is to manage your calls, messages, and calendar. If someone tries to take advantage of your time, interrupting your day, calling you before or after business hours or at inappropriate times, they may be imposing their lack of planning and organization into your precious time. Being related to toxic persons doesn't give them license to impinge on your life. The same rules apply. Set safe boundaries and don't engage until you are ready to do so. Just say no to the guilt and manipulation that these sorts of personalities wield like weapons of mass destruction.

I have one friend who calls it putting his mother and her dictatorial husband into "time out." He doesn't return their calls during work hours and only returns calls when he is feeling emotionally strong because this duo spews so much negativity and heaps criticism about everything he does in his life and that of his family. You don't have to put up with emotional abuse, period.

There are people in my life who are so dear to me, so trusted and valued, that I will take their call or return their text just about any time, even if I need to step out of a meeting. There are others whose calls I routinely let go to voicemail or leave their e-mails unanswered, even if I am available. You do not have time for people you do not trust or who want to dump their problems on you.

Recent research from the Department of Biological and Clinical Psychology at Friedrich Schiller University in Germany found that exposure to stimuli that cause strong negative emotions—the same kind of exposure you get when dealing with toxic people—caused subjects' brains to have a massive stress response.[106] To experience less bad stress in relationships, **STOP** spending time with people who bring you down. It's not you, it's them. They bring everyone else down, too.

Questions for Reflection

- Do you have any negative people in your life?
- How do you manage yourself so that those negative people do not suck the life out of you?
- What one step can you take to **STOP** spending time with people who bring you down?

CHAPTER 19

STOP and Smell the Roses with People You Love

I love spending time with my friends and family. The simplest things in life give me the most pleasure: cooking a good meal, enjoying my friends.
—Cindy Morgan

What would the famous correspondence between Thomas Jefferson and John Adams look like if they had e-mail, text messaging, and social media? We have a wonderful record of the two founding fathers and former presidents, who were friends early in their careers, bitter political enemies in the middle, and friends again toward the end of their lives. A letter would take weeks to arrive and people wrote letters as if they were writing an important document that might be turned into class for a grade. There were no spell checks or auto-correct tools.

Jefferson invented an ingenious early copy machine with a mechanical arm that would make a duplicate copy of his letter with an additional feather quill pen and ink. Because he saved the letters from Adams and a copy of his own, we have a fully documented account of their heartfelt correspondence, eloquently written. The exhibit below is an excerpt of correspondence between the two founding fathers toward the end of their life, after they put their differences aside and renewed their friend-ship.

Correspondence between Jefferson and Adams

1812, January 21: Jefferson to Adams

A letter from you calls up recollections very dear to my mind. It carries me back to the times when, beset with difficulties and dangers, we were fellow laborers in the same cause, struggling for what is most valuable to man, his right of self-government. Laboring always at the same oar, with some wave ever ahead threatening to overwhelm us and yet passing harmless under our bark, we knew not how, we rode through the storm with heart and hand, and made a happy port. . . . But whither is senile garrulity leading me? Into politics, of which I have taken final leave. I think little of them, and say less. I have given up newspapers in exchange for Tacitus and Thucydides, for Newton and Euclid; and I find myself much the happier. Sometimes indeed I look back to former occurrences, in remembrance of our old friends and fellow laborers, who have fallen before us. Of the signers of the Declaration of Independence I see now living not more than half a dozen on your side of the Potomac, and, on this side, myself alone. You and I have been wonderfully spared, and myself with remarkable health, and a considerable activity of body and mind. I am on horseback 2 every day; visit 3. or 4. hours of every day; visit 3. or 4. times a year a possession I have 90 miles distant, performing the winter journey on horseback. I walk little however; a single mile being too much for me; and I live in the midst of my grandchildren, one of whom has lately promoted me to be a great grandfather.

1812, February 3 (13 days later), Adams to Jefferson

Your Memoranda of the past, your Sense of the present and Prospect for the Future seem to be well founded, as far as I see. But the Latter i.e. the Prospect of the Future, will depend on the Union: and how is that Union to be preserved? *Concordia Res parvae crescunt, Discordia Maximae dilabuntur. . .* The Union is still to me an Object of as much

Anxiety as ever Independence was. To this I have sacrificed my Popularity in New England and yet what Treatment do I still receive from the Randolphs and Sheffeys of Virginia. By the Way are not these Eastern Shore Men? My Senectutal Loquacity has more than retaliated your Senile Garrulity. . . . I walk every fair day, sometimes 3 or 4 miles. Ride now and then but very rarely more than ten or fifteen Miles. . . . I have the Start of you in Age by at least ten Years: but you are advanced to the Rank of a Great Grandfather before me.[107]

This wonderful correspondence went back and forth until 1826 when Jefferson and Adams both died, amazingly on the same day, even more amazingly on July 4, 1826, fifty years to the day of the signing of the Declaration of Independence.

Do you feel like you have time to sit down and write a long letter to a dear friend, or even a short letter? Expressing thought in a short, concise, and meaningful way takes careful thought and organization.

Investing in relationships can be greatly enhanced by thoughtful correspondence. The art of the handwritten note is a dying one in this digital age. Margaret Shepherd, in her delightful little book, *The Art of the Handwritten Note*, writes, "The handwritten note has so many virtues that you ought to reach for pen and paper first, before you pick up the phone or move the mouse. In contrast to a phone call, a handwritten note doesn't arrive demanding to be read when you've just sat down to dinner; it courteously lets you know who sent it even before you open it; you won't be annoyed by the sounds coming from the pens of compulsive note-writers at the next table in your favorite restaurant."[108]

Correspondence is a great way to express your fondness for the ones you love when you are absent from them. Even a well-placed thoughtful phone call, e-mail, or text message can be meaningful when you are not with your friend or loved one. But there is nothing as special as being together in person, enjoying time together with all your senses activated, reading the meaning in the eyes, the smile, the touch of a hand, and the expression of body language.

I am so grateful for my family and friends. First, I am fortunate to have wonderful parents, Bruce and Judy Parmenter, who at the time of this writing are enjoying good health and a well-lived life after sixty-five years of marriage at age eighty-three. They live in Urbana, Illinois, not far from my sister Patti, who as a nurse practitioner serves as their personal healthcare advisor. I have three sisters, Linda, Cindi, and Patti, and a brother, Todd. I am the youngest of all five. I appreciate their spouses and children and grandchildren and always look forward to our times together.

I am the luckiest guy in the world to be married to Sherry. She is so loving, kind, and encouraging to me. She is one of the sweetest people I have ever met, and many people agree. She keeps me going when times get tough, and I love spending time together just about every day.

Together we have seven children—Natalie, Austin, Jordan, Lauren, Kelsey, Paige, and Aden. They are separated by twenty-two years from the oldest to the youngest, and Natalie and her husband David have five boys. Lauren is married to Charlie. As of this writing, two more grandchildren are on their way. Each child is unique and has a personality unlike the others. In fact, we have observed with our children what a study published in the *Journal of Social Psychology and Personality Science* found, which is that our personalities are pretty much set for life by the first grade.[109] We enjoy every opportunity we have to spend time with our family, which isn't easy as many are separated by geography. I could tell hilarious and heartwarming stories about each of our children, but that would take another book. Maybe someday I will write that book.

I have made many friends over the years and keep in touch with many of them on a regular basis even though they live all over the world. Some of my best friends were work colleagues and fellow students, and even though we have moved on to other jobs and graduated from school, we remain in touch. When you work side-by-side for long periods of time and accomplish meaningful achievements together, with mutual respect and enjoyment of one another's company, great bonds of friendship are formed, like Jefferson and Adams.

The last five years of my life have been the most exciting. Sherry and I married in 2011, and I moved from Chicago, Illinois, to my wife's hometown of Nashville, Tennessee, and now consider myself a Southerner. This is our home together now. The Nashville area has so much to offer and is so much more than country music. I love all kinds of music, including country, and it can all be found on a stage from a small coffee shop to a large concert venue. In fact, Nashville has more than 150 live music venues, so Sherry and I could literally go out almost every other night in our town. More surprising to some is that the Nashville area is home to more healthcare companies than any city in the United States. I work in the healthcare industry and have met many industry professionals here and have made some terrific friends.

Sherry and I love to travel and have a long list of places that we plan to visit, but there is no place like home. Perhaps that's why *The Wizard of Oz* is Sherry's favorite movie of all time.

Also in late 2011, I joined Evolent Health as employee No. 9. Evolent is a start-up healthcare services company that helps leading health systems build successful population health-management organizations. We now employ more than one thousand Evolenteers, and I am so humbled to be part of a company filled with positive, can-do, smart, motivated professionals on a mission to change the health of the nation by changing the way healthcare is delivered. That is the mission of the company and permeates everything we do, every day. I have made many wonderful new friends at Evolent and wish that everyone had the chance to work with friends in pursuit of a common goal. There is nothing as rewarding from a career perspective.

Our three founders, Frank Williams, our chief executive officer; Seth Blackley, our president; and Tom Peterson, our chief operating officer, set the positive tone of our company. We joke about them being three men and a truck back in 2011, but their vision and commitment and caring about the employees, clients, and ultimately patients who we serve have led to the formation of many relationships that will last a long, long time.

We all suffer. It is inevitable that tough times will come our way. Some of these events are tragic, like the loss of a child to disease or violence. Some are devastating, like the loss of a job and resulting financial crisis. No matter the suffering, there is no replacement for a supportive community of people who care for and about us. Sometimes this support comes from family and/or from friends in a supportive community such as a local church.

These relationships are not only necessary for the extra help that we need during tough times, but actually change the physiological response in our brain. Jim Coan is a social neuroscientist who has found that gestures, such as holding the hands of loved ones, reduces the brain's perception of threat. In several studies he has found that when our loved ones are near, we react less to stress—and critically, we are less likely to activate structures in the brain that govern our hormonal response to stress.[110]

I could go on and on about the people I know and love, but suffice it to say that I sincerely believe that our mental and physical health is directly related to the relationships we nurture in life.

Stopping to smell the roses is a metaphor for not missing the beauty in life, because we are too busy getting to our destination. Life is much more about the journey than the destination. The best way to manage stress is to spend time with the ones you love—quality and quantity time, face-to-face if possible, as often as possible. When we **STOP** to smell the roses with the ones we love, joyous emotions are evoked and well-being is enhanced for each person in the relationship.

Questions for Reflection

- Think of a recent time when you stopped to smell the roses with someone you love. What was that like?
- When was the last time you sent a handwritten note?
- Who would love to hear from you today?

CHAPTER 20

STOP Devaluing Yourself

The worst loneliness is to not be comfortable with yourself.

—Mark Twain

You and I are unique. There is no one alive, or who has ever lived, or who will ever live, who is just like you. Every person has a special gift to give that can make the world a better place. I believe that everyone can experience well-being despite suffering in life. Well-being is more a state of mind than a physical state.

Many have been raised in a harsh environment with an abusive parent. The messages of not being good enough play over and over in the minds of many people, because of the way they were raised or disappointments in life. Erasing these recordings and imprints on the brain are difficult and, for many, require some structured professional help.

My father's vocation was that of a pastor, a college professor, and a marriage and family counselor. I have been fortunate to grow up in a positive, loving family. My father recognized early in his ministry and counseling practice that issues of self-esteem were at the root of so many triggering events that brought clients to his counseling room. He was so convinced of the role of self-esteem that he wrote a book on the topic more than thirty years ago called *What the Bible Says about Self-Esteem*. This book was written as a daily devotional guide for 365 days of the year where each chapter began with a verse of the Bible that highlighted how unique, special, and loved we are from God's perspective.

Feelings of inadequacy, guilt, and shame that result from sustained negative messages or mistakes in life have detrimental health effects. According to Michael Lewis, PhD, "Shame is the quintessential human emotion," and Donald Nathanson, MD, says, "All extravagant behaviors are reactions to it."[111]

Marilyn Sorensen, PhD, author of *Breaking the Chain of Low Self-Esteem*, says, "Early in life, individuals develop an internalized view of themselves as adequate or inadequate within the world. Children who are continually criticized, severely punished, neglected, abandoned, or in other ways abused or mistreated get the message that they do not 'fit' in the world—that they are inadequate, inferior or unworthy."[112]

The field of positive psychology is growing in popularity in great part due to the work of Martin Seligman and his groundbreaking work on the science of happiness. Seligman teaches new ways to think about self-worth by focusing on the positives. "Real, lasting happiness comes from focusing on one's personal strengths rather than weaknesses—and working with them to improve all aspects of one's life."[113]

Many wellness experts who help employers develop cultures of health in the workplace, like my friend Rose Gantner, recognize that self-esteem is at the heart of well-being. She incorporates the components of positive psychology into wellness programs, recognizing that improved exercise and nutrition are not enough to address issues like depression.

There is no easy, simple formula or solution for dealing with low self-esteem. The following tips from John Grohol, PsyD offer a good start:[114]

- Take a self-esteem inventory.
- Set realistic expectations.
- Set aside perfection and grab a hold of accomplishments . . . and mistakes.
- Explore yourself.
- Be willing to adjust your own self-image.
- Stop comparing yourself to others.

The messages we internalize can rob us of self-worth if we allow them, and sometimes we send messages that can negatively impact others. I am reminded of the teaching of my first sales trainers who said: "Never tell anyone to go to hell, because they won't go just because you told them to and they will never forget that you told them to."

I am not sure where I found the following story, but I share it because it is a beautiful reminder of the hurt that we experience and sometimes inflict on the ones we love the most.

A frail old man went to live with his son, daughter-in-law, and four-year-old grandson.
The old man's hands trembled, his eyesight was blurred, and his step faltered.

The family ate together at the table. But the elderly grandfather's shaky hands and failing sight made eating difficult. Peas rolled off his spoon onto the floor.
When he grasped the glass, milk spilled on the tablecloth.

The son and daughter-in-law became irritated with the mess.
"We must do something about Father," said the son.
"I've had enough of his spilled milk, noisy eating, and food on the floor."

So the husband and wife set a small table in the corner.
There, Grandfather ate alone while the rest of the family enjoyed dinner.
Since Grandfather had broken a dish or two, his food was served in a wooden bowl.

When the family glanced in Grandfather's direction, sometimes he had a tear in his eye as he sat alone.

Still, the only words the couple had for him were sharp admonitions when he dropped a fork or spilled food.

The four-year-old watched it all in silence.

One evening before supper, the father noticed his son playing with wood scraps on the floor.
He asked the child sweetly, "What are you making?"

Just as sweetly, the boy responded, "Oh, I am making a little bowl for you and Mama to eat your food in when I grow up."
The four-year-old smiled and went back to work.

The words so struck the parents that they were speechless. Then tears started to stream down their cheeks. Though no word was spoken, both knew what must be done.

That evening the husband took Grandfather's hand and gently led him back to the family table.

For the remainder of his days he ate every meal with the family. And for some reason, neither husband nor wife seemed to care any longer when a fork was dropped, milk spilled, or the tablecloth soiled.

You are awesome! We all make mistakes, we all have negative experiences and have been told we are not good enough. There are many fine resources to help you discover and apply your strengths, including Marcus Buckingham and Donald Clifton's book *Now Discover Your Strengths: How to Develop Your Talents and Those of the People You Manage* as well as gift inventories that can help you find your unique gifts.[115]

Amy Cuddy, in her book *Presence: Bringing Your Boldest Self to Your Biggest Challenges,*[116] and in her famous TED Talk, describes how she overcame a traumatic automobile accident where her IQ dropped two standard deviations. For her whole life her identity was tied up in being smart, and now she was devastated that she could not keep up academically. She wanted to hide. She felt like she did not belong. She devalued herself. In spite of her fears and doubts, she struggled mightily through college and graduate school. With the inspiration of a professor she learned how to "fake it until she became it" and now is a psychologist and associate professor at Harvard Business School and known worldwide for her work on how people judge and influence each other and themselves. She could have cowered in fear and disappointment, but instead she made herself big and overcame. I highly recommend her TED Talk on www.ted.com called "Your Body Language Shapes Who You Are,"[117] which features her research and her personal story. The talk has gone viral with over two million views, and her story has inspired many, including me.

Edward Hallowell, MD, in his book *Shine* writes, "Smart is overrated. Talent is overrated. Breeding, Ivy League education, sophistication, wit, eloquence and good looks—they matter but they're all overrated. What really matters is what you do with what you have."[118]

Adam Grant, in his book *Originals: How Nonconformists Move the World*, says that, "Although child prodigies are often rich in both talent and ambition, what holds them back from moving the world forward is they don't learn to be original."[119] Grant tells stories about how great change was brought about in the world by reluctant but original people like Dr. Martin Luther King Jr. You have the most important ingredient to make a difference in the world, your own originality.

My friend Kevin Garrett is an original and a nonconformist. He photographed the art I produced for the cover of this book, took my author's photo, and took his portfolio to an art director for a firm that did corporate work for Fortune 500 companies. It was shortly after 9/11, and Kevin's entire portfolio was based on his work as a travel photographer, concentrating in the Caribbean. The art director looked at his book, and then handed it back to him, commenting, "Nice work."

"So are you going to hire me?" Kevin asked.

"Your pictures are gorgeous, but what do they have to do with shooting factory tours and products?" the man asked.

"If I can capture all the motion and energy in these shots, I know I can do what you need," Kevin replied. "Give me something small that you don't really have a lot riding on. If I mess it up, I won't ever ask you for a job again."

What he didn't say was that he had a wife and two young sons and was at a point where he felt pressure to shift his career direction, given the slump in travel at the time.

The art director agreed and gave him a small job to shoot that week. Kevin ended up getting thousands of dollars' worth of work from that client and still works for him today. He got those results because he refused to devalue his talents simply because he couldn't show samples of that particular kind of work right at that moment.

Make no mistake. No matter your lot in life, no matter the suffering you have experienced, you have something inside of you that is very special. The great poet Ralph Waldo Emerson wrote, "Every man I meet is my superior in some way. In that, I learn of him."

Give yourself more credit, do something with what you have, and **STOP** devaluing yourself.

Questions for Reflection

- What things in your life are you most thankful for?
- What would people that know you best say are some of your strengths?
- Who values you the most in life?

CHAPTER 21

STOP Reading This Book
and Get On with Your Life

You see, George, you've really had a wonderful life.
—*Clarence,* It's a Wonderful Life

Well, there you have it. I hope this book has given you at least one idea of something to **STOP** in your life, some behavior that, if set aside, would evoke well-being and joy. Your health, your work, and your life could benefit from doing less. We live in a frenzied, chaotic world and the increased speed and enhancements in technology, with all their benefits, will certainly escalate the pace and proliferate distractions that compete for our attention on a daily basis. Well-being and joy are threatened every moment of every day if we are unconscious. Take a deep breath and reflect on what you can **STOP** in your life so that you experience more of the emotion of joy and enjoy a sense of well-being.

So how do you get motivated to change certain behaviors in your life? You could try traditional behavioral modification and deploy rewards and punishment. For many years, behaviorism was considered the best way to influence behavior by setting up a system to reward good behavior and extinguish bad behavior by ignoring it or establishing a penalty. It is difficult to make a mule move if it doesn't want to move, so you could coax it with a carrot (the incentive) or whack it with a stick (the penalty). Carrots and sticks have become an often-used metaphor for incentives and penalties. Behavioral science teaches us that because we have a bias called "loss aversion"—meaning we place greater value on avoiding loss than experiencing gain—carrots work a little better than sticks.

In my work with employer wellness programs, sometimes we use a combination of carrots and sticks to increase participation in activities like completing a health assessment. We call this combination a frozen carrot, because it carries an incentive but can still be used for a little whack.

The problem with carrots and sticks is that they are only extrinsic motivation tools. We have learned that extrinsic rewards work okay to illicit very specific, small, and short-term behavior changes, such as giving a gift card to an employee as an incentive to complete a health assessment and to raise their cost if they fail to comply—that is the frozen carrot. These tools, however, do very little to influence lasting behavior change. Once you stop feeding the mule carrots or whacking him with a frozen carrot, he goes right back to the old behavior of stubbornness.

As discussed, changing habits is much more difficult. To change habits, you need to change routines and often rewards as well. These tools may be helpful to start us traveling down the right road as we begin a journey of change, but in order to achieve lasting change we need intrinsic motivation. In other words, if you really want to change, and you want that change to last, the best way is to be driven by a strong sense of purpose.

Pursuit of purpose leads to the freedom of the mind that evokes a greater sense of joy and well-being. In his book *Drive: The Surprising Truth About What Motivates Us*, Daniel Pink describes intrinsic motivators of human behavior with the three powerful forces of autonomy, mastery, and purpose.[120] We all want autonomy, yet many of the behaviors we need to **STOP** are holding us back from being autonomous and masters of our chosen pursuit.

If we have raw talent and the aptitude to pursue a purposeful endeavor, it will take a lot of time. Malcom Gladwell popularized the 10,000-hour principle that suggests that natural ability requires a huge investment of time in order to manifest.[121] Gladwell suggests that it takes 10,000 hours to become an expert in any chosen endeavor, assuming you have the talent or aptitude to be developed.[122] In order to free up the time needed to pursue your passion, you may need to **STOP**, do some slow thinking, and go to the lookout tower to objectively assess your behavior and determine what to **STOP**. Then, tune up your behaviors using the suggestions in this book to start working on your purpose in life.

The most compelling intrinsic motivator of our behavior, according to Pink, is purpose. He writes, "It's our nature to seek purpose. But the nature is now being revealed and expressed on a scale that is demographically unprecedented and, until recently, scarcely imaginable. The consequences could rejuvenate our businesses and remake our world."[123] Viktor Frankl, in his 1946 best seller *Man's Search for Meaning*, describes how he survived the horrors of Nazi death camps by holding on to the purpose of his life. He went on to write the book that would go on to not only sell more than 12 million copies, but to be named one of the ten most influential books of all time. Frankl wrote, "Those who have a 'why' to live, can bear with almost any 'how.'"

Adam Grant, in his book *Originals: How Non-Conformists Move the World*, unpacks in detail the surprising influences behind some of the world's greatest originals from T. S. Elliot to Dr. Martin Luther King to Thomas Edison.[124] Grant says that "Ultimately, the people who choose to champion originality propel us forward. They feel the same fear, the same doubt as the rest of us. What sets them apart is that they take action anyway. They know in their hearts that failing would yield less regret than failing to try." My hope for you is that you tap into your originality, find your purpose, take time to think slowly about it, and then go for it with all your passion. Changes are good. If you find your purpose and passion and focus on it fully, you will not only reduce your stress and enhance your joy, but you will give something of great value to others. Most lives that are lived with meaning and purpose are not selfish, they help others as beautifully described in Adam Grant's book *Give and Take: Why Helping Others Drives Our Success*.[125] Is there something keeping you from your purposeful pursuit?

One of my favorite classes in the University of Chicago Booth School of Business MBA program was a course taught in London by Professor Ayelet Fishbach on negotiation. One of the principles of winning a negotiation calls for you to remove yourself emotionally from the outcome. For instance, if you fall in love with a certain purchase, a house, or a position in a business transaction, you will likely pay more than if you are willing to walk away.

One of the ways to remove yourself emotionally from a negotiation—or anything in life—is to go to the lookout tower or balcony. Fishbach taught us to imagine ourselves in the balcony of a theatre, looking down on the action below as a detached observer, not as an actor in the play. By doing so, we gain a new perspective. We can imagine this out-of-body experience and ask questions objectively. Not only does this exercise help in negotiation, it helps you evaluate your life so that you can give your life a proper tune-up.

From your lookout tower, looking down on your life, what behaviors could you **STOP** that free up time, free up energy, improve your health, improve your relationships, and ultimately improve your performance?

These are the good old days. *Carpe diem*—seize the day. One of my favorite songs was written by one of my favorite songwriters, Jeffrey Steele. Jeffrey and his cowriter Steve Robson said more in the lines of "My Wish," recorded by Rascal Flatts, than I have said in this book. Give it a listen when you have a chance. I end this book with my wish for you, that through a reflective assessment of your life, you will **STOP** whatever it is that is holding you back and experience joy and well-being as a result.

Questions for Reflection

- What is your purpose in life?
- What things in your life, if you **STOP** right now, would enhance your well-being?
- What is your wish for your life?

Acknowledgments

Pit Crew

Like tuning up your car or behavior, writing a book requires slow thinking and a good pit crew. Writing ***STOP!*** was a team effort. There are many who deserve special recognition. Echo Garrett was my pit-crew boss and mentor. She has been an amazing writing coach and content editor who urged me to link the personal and professional experiences from my life to the research and academic perspectives. Dr. Gene Harker and Shawn Mathis have been personal mentors and writing coaches and have willingly read early and late manuscripts. I am also indebted to Annika Jaspers, who took a respite from her world travels to serve as copy editor.

Kevin Garrett spent an afternoon and the following morning with me shooting photos for the cover art, back cover photo, and inside photo. We had a wonderful time together and I found out firsthand why he is a world-class professional photographer and an all-around great guy. He is an original, and I included one of his stories of grit in the book.

The stop sign and background on the cover are original hand-painted oil-paint art by Amanda Hope Cook. Mandy, who is my wife Sherry's first cousin, is from a family of fine artists and one of the finest artists I've come across. Hector Sanchez is responsible for the overall cover design and has also been a great advisor and coach. David Pfendler is responsible for the illustrations in the book and did an amazing job based mostly on my descriptions and chicken scratches.

The folks at BookLogix in Alpharetta, Georgia, have been wonderful to work with. Brette Sember provided quality indexing work.

Friends, Family, and Colleagues

My wife Sherry allowed me to invest time that otherwise could have been spent with her so that I could write this book. She also gave me great ideas and read early versions gladly. I would like to thank all of my friends and colleagues, particularly those at Evolent Health and Vanderbilt University Medical Center, for providing an opportunity to work with the best and brightest in the healthcare industry.

I am indebted to my family for loving and accepting me with all my flaws and shortcomings. I am especially inspired by my father, Bruce Parmenter, who instilled in me a love for writing and who set the example, and my mother, Judy Parmenter, for loving me unconditionally.

My Favorite Books

The following is a list of some of my favorite books, many of which are referenced in this book and all of which have influenced my thinking. Not all of these books relate to the topic of **STOP** directly or even indirectly, but they have influenced my thinking. The Bible has influenced my thinking more than any other book. I highly recommend all of these books and list the primary titles, along with the author's name. You can easily find them by searching online with these words. I'm sure there are others that I have left off and will add to future editions of *STOP!*.

- ***Presence:*** *Bringing Your Boldest Self to Your Biggest Challenges* by Amy Cuddy
- ***The Wisdom of Bees:*** *What the Hive Can Teach Business about Leadership, Efficiency, and Growth* by Michael O'Malley
- ***Good to Great:*** *Why Some Companies Make the Leap . . . and Others Don't* by Jim Collins
- ***Freakonomics:*** *A Rogue Economist Explores the Hidden Side of Everything* by Steven D. Levitt and Stephen J. Dubner
- ***Who Killed HealthCare?:*** *America's $2 Trillion Medical Problem—and the Consumer-Driven Cure* by Regina Herzlinger
- ***Redefining Health Care:*** *Creating Value-Based Competition on Results* by Michael E. Porter and Elizabeth Olmsted Teisberg
- ***Think and Grow Rich*** by Napoleon Hill
- ***The Prophet*** by Kahlil Gibran
- ***How to Win Friends & Influence People*** by Dale Carnegie

- ***The 7 Habits of Highly Effective People:*** *Powerful Lessons in Personal Change* by Stephen R. Covey
- ***Nudge:*** *Improving Decisions About Health, Wealth, and Happiness* by Richard Thaler and Cass Sunstein
- ***Thinking, Fast and Slow*** by Daniel Kahneman
- ***Predictably Irrational:*** *The Hidden Forces that Shape Our Decisions* by Dan Ariely
- ***A Whole New Mind:*** *Why Right-Brainers Will Rule the Future* by Daniel H. Pink
- ***Drive:*** *The Surprising Truth About What Motivates Us* by Daniel H. Pink
- ***The Power of Habit:*** *Why We Do What We Do in Life and Business* by Charles Duhigg
- ***The Total Money Makeover:*** *A Proven Plan for Financial Fitness* by Dave Ramsey
- ***The Tipping Point:*** *How Little Things Can Make a Big Difference* by Malcom Gladwell
- ***Outliers:*** *The Story of Success* by Malcom Gladwell
- ***David and Goliath:*** *Underdogs, Misfits, and the Art of Battling Giants* by Malcom Gladwell
- ***Blink:*** *The Power of Thinking Without Thinking* by Malcom Gladwell
- ***Shine:*** *Using Brain Science to Get the Best from Your People* by Edward M. Hallowell
- ***Leadership Insight:*** *The New Psychology of Grit, Success & Well-Being* by Gene Harker, MD, PhD
- ***Pause Points:*** *The Mindful Pursuit of Health & Well-Being* by Gene Harker, MD, PhD and Curt Smith
- ***My Orange Duffel Bag:*** *A Journey to Radical Change* by Sam Bracken and Echo Garrett

- ***Getting Things Done:*** *The Art of Stress-Free Productivity* by David Allen

- ***Influence:*** *The Psychology of Persuasion* by Robert B. Cialdini

- ***Workplace Wellness:*** *Performance with a Purpose* by Dr. Rose Karlo Gantner, EdD

- ***Margin:*** *Restoring Emotional, Physical, Financial, and Time Reserves to Overloaded Lives* by Richard Swenson

- ***Mindwise:*** *Why We Misunderstand What Others Think, Believe, Feel, and Want* by Nick Epley

- ***The Art of the Handwritten Note:*** *A Guide to Reclaiming Civilized Communication* by Margaret Shepherd

- ***The Situational Leader:*** *The Other 59 Minutes* by Dr. Paul Hersey

- ***Self-Esteem:*** *A Proven Program of Cognitive Techniques for Assessing, Improving & Maintaining Your Self-Esteem* by Matthew McKay, PhD and Patrick Fanning

- ***What the Bible Says About Self-Esteem*** by Bruce Parmenter

- ***The Resilient Pastor:*** *Ten Principles for Developing Pastoral Resilience* by Mark Searby

- ***Well Designed Life:*** *10 Lessons in Brain Science & Design Thinking for a Mindful, Healthy & Purposeful Life* by Kyra Bobinet, MD, MPH

- ***Why Smart People Make Big Money Mistakes and How to Correct Them:*** *Lessons from the Life-Changing Science of Behavioral Economics* by Gary Belsky and Thomas Gilovich

- ***Irrationality in Health Care:*** *What Behavioral Economics Reveals About What We Do and Why* by Douglas Hough

- ***Less:*** *Accomplishing More by Doing Less* by Marc Lesser

- ***Search Inside Yourself:*** *The Unexpected Path to Achieving Success, Happiness (and World Peace)* by Chade-Meng Tan

- ***Your Brain at Work:*** *Strategies for Overcoming Distractions, Regaining Focus, and Working Smarter All Day Long* by David Rock

- ***The Art of Possibility:*** *Transforming Professional and Personal Life* by Rosamund Stone Zander and Benjamin Zander
- ***Man's Search for Meaning*** by Viktor Frankl
- ***The Rise of Superman:*** *Decoding the Science of Ultimate Human Performance* by Steven Kotler
- ***Give and Take:*** *Why Helping Others Drives Our Success* by Adam M. Grant
- ***Originals:*** *How Non-Conformists Move the World* by Adam M. Grant
- ***One Piece of Paper:*** *The Simple Approach to Powerful, Personal Leadership* by Mike Figliuolo
- ***The Obstacle Is the Way:*** *The Timeless Art of Turning Trials into Triumph* by Ryan Holiday
- ***Now, Discover Your Strengths*** by Marcus Buckingham and Donald O. Clifton
- ***Authentic Happiness:*** *Using the New Positive Psychology to Realize Your Potential for Lasting Fulfillment* by Martin E. P. Seligman
- ***Learned Optimism:*** *How to Change Your Mind and Your Life* by Martin E. P. Seligman
- ***Flourish:*** *A Visionary New Understanding of Happiness and Well-being* by Martin E. P. Seligman
- ***Persuasive Technology***: *Using Computers to Change What We Think and Do* by B. J. Fogg
- ***Flow:*** *The Psychology of Optimal Experience* by Mihaly Csikszent-mihalyi
- ***The Power of Full Engagement:*** *Managing Energy, Not Time, Is the Key to High Performance and Personal Renewal* by Jim Loehr and Tony Schwartz
- ***Freedom of Simplicity:*** *Finding Harmony in a Complex World* by Richard J. Foster
- ***Stumbling on Happiness*** by Daniel Gilbert

- ***The Purpose Driven Life:*** *What on Earth Am I Here For?* by Rick Warren

- ***Mindless Eating:*** *Why We Eat More Than We Think* by Brian Wansink

- ***All I Really Need to Know I Learned in Kindergarten*** by Robert Fulghum

- ***Total Leadership:*** *Be a Better Leader, Have a Richer Life* by Stewart Friedman

- ***Leading the Life You Want:*** *Skills for Integrating Work and Life* by Stewart Friedman

- ***Focus:*** *The Hidden Driver of Excellence* by Daniel Goleman

- ***The Progress Principle:*** *Using Small Wins to Ignite Joy, Engagement, and Creativity at Work* by Teresa Amabile

- ***The Why of Work:*** *How Great Leaders Build Abundant Organizations That Win* by David Ulrich

- ***Start with Why:*** *How Great Leaders Inspire Everyone to Take Action* by Simon Sinik

- ***Living Forward:*** *A Proven Plan to Stop Drifting and Get the Life You Want* by Michael Hyatt and Daniel Harkavy

- ***Shave 10 Hours off Your Workweek:*** *4 Proven Strategies to Create More Margin for the Things That Matter Most* by Michael Hyatt

Additional Resources

If you would like to learn more about resources that are available to assist you on your journey to enhance joy, reduce bad stress, enjoy greater well-being, and **STOP** behaviors that keep you from pursuing your purpose in life, please visit:

www.ericparmenter.com

This website provides more information about me including my blog, video clips of presentations, downloadable articles, recommendations on apps and digital devices, and links to other great resources.

About the Author

Eric Parmenter is established as a national expert on the impact of healthcare reform on healthcare providers and is a respected thought leader in the hospital health-system industry. A consultant with deep experience in health-plan strategy, design, prevention care, and productivity and behavioral economics, Eric serves as the market president for Tennessee and vice president of Employer Solutions for Evolent Health. A former principal with Towers Watson, he has worked in the employee-benefits business for thirty-plus years as an advisor to hospital and health-system clients, developing health benefit and prevention-care strategies that align with the health system's population-health business. Eric focuses on improving the poor health of healthcare workers and professionals as a first step to improving patient satisfaction and quality outcomes. He frequently speaks about the direct link between improving healthcare workers' health and boosting patient satisfaction and quality outcomes.

Eric M. Parmenter, CLU, ChFC, LUTCF, RHU, REBC, CEBS, SPHR, MBA

Eric has authored more than twenty articles on employee benefit topics including "Healthcare Benefit Crisis—Ten Years Later" in 2015, "Choice Architecture—a Tool for Ratcheting up Benefit and Wellness Results," "eACOs—The Health Plan of the Future," and "Healthcare Benefit Crisis." A member of several "Who's Who" lists for business executives, Eric graduated from the University of Illinois with a BA in psychology and earned his MBA from the University of Chicago Booth School of Business.

Eric lives in Nashville, Tennessee, with his wife Sherry and enjoys travel related to history, architecture, and baseball. Together, Eric and Sherry have seven children and five grandsons. He has been a volunteer docent for the Frank Lloyd Wright Preservation Trust.

References

Introduction

[1] Pamela Wible, "TEDMED Talk: Why Doctors Kill Themselves," Ideal Medical Care, March 23, 2016, http://www.idealmedicalcare.org/blog/tedmed-talk-why-doctors-kill-themselves/.

[2] Daniel Kahneman, *Thinking, Fast and Slow* (New York: Farrar, Straus and Giroux, 2013).

[3] Charles Duhigg, *The Power of Habit* (New York: Random House, 2012). The following four citations are from this source.

[4] Duhigg, *The Power of Habit*.

[5] Duhigg, *The Power of Habit*.

[6] Duhigg, *The Power of Habit*.

[7] Duhigg, *The Power of Habit*.

[8] Ryan Collins, "Exercise, Depression, and the Brain," Healthline, March 29, 2016, http://www.healthline.com/health/depression/exercise#1.

[9] "Nicotine," *Psychology Today*, December 27, 2015, https://www.psychologytoday.com/conditions/nicotine.

[10] Peter Valdes, "Worst drivers: teens, doctors, lawyers," CNN Money, November 18, 2004, http://money.cnn.com/2003/10/30/pf/autos/bad_drivers/.

[11] Eric Parmenter, "An Unhealthy Workforce," *HR Pulse*, Fall 2011.

[12] "11 Common Stress Triggers," item 2, "Money Issues," *Whole Living: Body+Soul in Balance*, http://www.wholeliving.com/136234/11-common-stress-triggers/@center/136756/stress-relief-your-guided-tour#135951.

[13] Stephen Feller, "Most U.S. adults lead unhealthy lifestyle, study says," UPI, March 21, 2016, http://www.upi.com/Health_News/2016/03/21/Most-US-adults-lead-unhealthy-lifestyle-study-says/4781458588581/.

[14] *Merriam-Webster Online*, s.v. "joy," accessed May 4, 2016, http://www.merriam-webster.com/dictionary/joy.

[15] Doc and Howard Martin, *The HeartMath Solution: The Institute of HeartMath's Revolutionary Program for Engaging the Power of the Heart's Intelligence* (New York: HarperCollins Publishers, 1999).

[16] *Wikipedia*, s.v. "Telos (philosophy)," last modified April 25, 2016, https://en.wikipedia.org/wiki/Telos_(philosophy).

[17] *Wikipedia*, s.v. "Techne," last modified January 19, 2016, https://en.wikipedia.org/wiki/Techne.

[18] *Wikipedia*, s.v. "Techne," https://en.wikipedia.org/wiki/Techne.

[19] Jim Collins, *Good to Great* (New York: HarperBusiness, 2001).

Chapter 1

[20] "Eating to boost energy," *Harvard Health Publications* from Harvard Medical School, July 26, 2011, http://www.health.harvard.edu/healthbeat/eating-to-boost-energy.

[21] "How Tilapia Is a More Unhealthy Food Than Bacon," *Eat This Not That*, accessed May 4, 2016, http://www.eatthis.com/tilapia-is-worse-than-bacon. Subscription required for access.

[22] Brian Wansink, "Mindless Eating: Why We Eat More than We Think," accessed May 4, 2016, http://www.mindlesseating.org/.

Chapter 2

[23] Gene Harker, *Pause Points* (Bloomington, Indiana: Westbow Press, 2011).

[24] "Alcohol Facts and Statistics," National Institute on Alcohol Abuse and Alcoholism, last modified January 2016, http://www.niaaa.nih.gov/alcohol-health/overview-alcohol-consumption/alcohol-facts-and-statistics.

[25] "Alcohol Facts and Statistics," http://www.niaaa.nih.gov/alcohol-health/overview-alcohol-consumption/alcohol-facts-and-statistics.

[26] Al Mooney and Catherine Dold, *The Recovery Book: Answers to All Your Questions About Addiction and Alcoholism and Finding Health and Happiness in Sobriety* (New York: Workman Publishing, 1992).

[27] Center for Disease Control and Prevention, "Alcohol and Pregnancy," maintained by Office of the Associate Director for Communications, last modified February 2, 2016, http://www.cdc.gov/vitalsigns/fasd/.

[28] Arnold O. Beckman, *One Hundred Years of Excellence (Chemical Heritage Foundation Series in Innovation and Entrepreneurship)* (Philadelphia: Chemical Heritage Foundation, 2000).

[29] "History of the Beckman Institute," Beckman Institute at University of Illinois at Urbana-Champaign, accessed May 5, 2016, http://beckman.illinois.edu/about/beckman/history.

Chapter 3

[30] Health Parks Healthy People Central, "Forest bathing," Parks Victoria, accessed May 5, 2016, http://www.hphpcentral.com/article/forest-bathing.

[31] Lisa Fields, "Do You Have Sitting Disease?" *WebMD*, November 22, 2012, http://www.webmd.com/fitness-exercise/do-you-have-sitting-disease.

32 "Adult Obesity Facts," Centers for Disease Control and Prevention, last updated September 21, 2015, http://www.cdc.gov/obesity/data/adult.html.

33 Dr. Joseph Mercola, "How the Sugar Industry Hoodwinked You about the Dangers of Sugar, Using Big Tobacco Tactics," Mercola.com, December 1, 2012, http://articles.mercola.com/sites/articles/archive/2012/12/01/sugar-industry.aspx.

34 National Center for Biotechnology Information Database (PubMed ID: 21694556; accessed May 5, 2016), http://www.ncbi.nlm.nih.gov/pubmed/21694556.

35 Jim Loehr and Tony Schwartz, "The Making of a Corporate Athlete," *Harvard Business Review*, January 2001.

36 Jim Loehr and Tony Schwartz, *The Power of Full Engagement: Managing Energy, Not Time, Is the Key to Performance and Personal Renewal* (New York: Free Press, 2003).

Chapter 4

37 Lisa Firestone, "Benefits of Mindfulness," *Psychology Today*, March 6, 2013, https://www.psychologytoday.com/blog/compassion-matters/201303/benefits-mindfulness.

38 Sandra Bond, *Make Your Brain Smarter: Increase Your Brain's Creativity, Energy, and Focus* (New York: Simon and Schuster, 2013).

39 John Geirland, "Buddha on the Brain," *Wired*, February 1, 2016, http://www.wired.com/2006/02/dalai/.

40 Geirland, "Buddha on the Brain," http://www.wired.com/2006/02/dalai/.

41 National Center for Biotechnology Information Database (PMC ID: PMC3156028; accessed May 5, 2016), http://www.ncbi.nlm.nih.gov/pmc/articles/PMC3156028/.

42 National Center for Biotechnology Information Database (PMC ID: PMC2908186; accessed May 5, 2016), http://www.ncbi.nlm.nih.gov/pmc/articles/PMC2908186/.

43 National Center for Biotechnology Information Database, http://www.ncbi.nlm.nih.gov/pmc/articles/PMC2908186/.

44 National Center for Biotechnology Information Database, http://www.ncbi.nlm.nih.gov/pmc/articles/PMC2908186/.

45 Jim Loehr and Tony Schwartz, "The Making of a Corporate Athlete," *Harvard Business Review*, January 2001.

46 "Left Brain Vs Right Brain," UCMAS Mental Math Schools, accessed May 5, 2016, http://ucmas.ca/our-programs/whole-brain-development/left-brain-vs-right-brain/.

47 Daniel Pink, *A Whole New Mind* (New York: Penguin Group, 2006).

48 Stuart Heritage, "Bored of Mindfulness? Give Mindlessness a Try," *The Guardian*, June 12, 2015, http://www.theguardian.com/lifeandstyle/2015/jun/12/give-mindlessness-a-try.

[49] Joseph Stromberg, "The Benefits of Daydreaming," *Smithsonian*, April 3, 2012, http://www.smithsonianmag.com/science-nature/the-benefits-of-daydreaming-170189213/?no-ist.

Chapter 5

[50] Google dictionary, s.v. "nostalgia," accessed May 5, 2016, https://www.google.com/#q=nostalgia.

[51] Kerianne Doi, "'I Will Never Be Here Again': The Psychology of Nostalgia," The Moral Communities Project, June 8, 2014, http://moralcommunities.com/psychology-of-nostalgia/.

[52] Tarek Kerbag, "Nostalgia and Its Emotional, Spiritual, and Physical Benefits," Science in Our World: Certainty and Controversy (SC200) course website, October 26, 2012, http://www.personal.psu.edu/afr3/blogs/siowfa12/2012/10/nostalgia-and-its-emotional-spiritual-and-physical-benefits.html.

[53] Thorin Klosowski, "How to Use Nostalgia to Your Advantage (Instead of Getting Stuck)," *Lifehacker*, January 22, 2015, http://lifehacker.com/how-to-use-nostalgia-to-your-advantage-instead-of-gett-1681068093.

[54] Klowsowski, "How to Use Nostalgia to Your Advantage," http://lifehacker.com/how-to-use-nostalgia-to-your-advantage-instead-of-gett-1681068093.

[55] Homer, *The Odyssey* bk. 5.

[56] *Wikipedia*, s.v. "Achilles' heel," last modified March 14, 2016, https://en.wikipedia.org/wiki/Achilles%27_heel.

[57] "A Brief History," Unclaimed Baggage Center's website, accessed May 5, 2016, http://www.unclaimedbaggage.com/about/timeline/.

[58] Cameron Chardukian, "Why You Dwell on the Past and How to Stop," *Self-Improvement for Young Hustlers* (blog), November 12, 2013, http://cameronchardukian.com/how-to-stop-dwelling/.

[59] Ohio University, "Dwelling on stressful events can increase inflammation in the body, study finds," *Science Daily*, March 13, 2013, https://www.sciencedaily.com/releases/2013/03/130313182255.htm.

[60] Robin Hilmantel, "How to Stop Dwelling," Women's Health, *Prevention*, March 20, 2013, http://www.prevention.com/mind-body/emotional-health/moving-past-stressful-events.

[61] Terry Shea, "Art of the Design - 1940 Lincoln Continental," *Hemmings*, May 2015, http://www.hemmings.com/hcc/stories/2015/05/01/hmn_feature4.html. Photo courtesy of *Hemmings* Archives.

Chapter 6

[62] Kathleen Doheny, "Clutter Control: Is Too Much 'Stuff' Draining You?" *WebMD*, last reviewed June 19, 2008, http://www.webmd.com/a-to-z-guides/features/clutter-control.

[63] "Hoarding Fact Sheet," International OCD Foundation, accessed May 5, 2016, https://iocdf.org/wp-content/uploads/2014/10/Hoarding-Fact-Sheet.pdf.

64 Richard Foster, *Freedom of Simplicity* (New York: Harper & Row, 1981).

65 Kathleen Doheny, "Clutter Control: Is Too Much 'Stuff' Draining You?" *WebMD*, last reviewed June 19, 2008, http://www.webmd.com/a-to-z-guides/features/clutter-control.

Chapter 7

66 Richard Thaler and Cass Sunstein, *Nudge: Improving Decisions About Health, Wealth, and Happiness* (New York: Penguin Books, 2009).

67 Charles Duhigg, *The Power of Habit* (New York: Random House, 2012).

68 Duhigg, *The Power of Habit*.

Chapter 8

69 Sarah Williams, "Prioritizing Your Marketing Goals & Campaigns Using Lists," 816 New York, accessed May 5, 2016, http://816nyc.com/business-advice-andrew-carnegie-ignore/.

70 Henrik Edberg, "Andrew Carnegie's Top 4 Tips for Massive Success," *The Positivity Blog*, accessed May 5, 2016, http://www.positivityblog.com/index.php/2009/08/10/andrew-carnegies-top-4-tips-for-massive-success/.

71 "FOCUS: Achieving Your Highest Priorities™," Training & Consulting, Franklin Covey, accessed May 5, 2016, http://www.franklincovey.ca/FCCAWeb/aspx/train_focus.htm.

Chapter 9

72 Ray Williams, "Why goal setting doesn't work," *Psychology Today*, April 11, 2011, https://www.psychologytoday.com/blog/wired-success/201104/why-goal-setting-doesnt-work.

73 Eric Beech, "U.S. government says it lost $11.2 billion on GM bailout," Business, *Reuters*, April 30, 2014, http://www.reuters.com/article/us-autos-gm-treasury-idUSBREA3T0MR20140430.

74 Ray Williams, "Why goal setting doesn't work," *Psychology Today*, April 11, 2011, https://www.psychologytoday.com/blog/wired-success/201104/why-goal-setting-doesnt-work.

75 Williams, "Why goal setting doesn't work," https://www.psychologytoday.com/blog/wired-success/201104/why-goal-setting-doesnt-work.

Chapter 10

76 Michael T. Robinson, "The Generations - What Generation Are You?" Career Planner website, accessed May 5, 2016, http://www.careerplanner.com/Career-Articles/Generations.cfm.

77 Johnathan Koomey, "The Computing Trend That Will Change Everything," Business Reports, *MIT Technology Review*, April 9, 2012, http://www.technologyreview.com/news/427444/the-computing-trend-that-will-change-everything/. Subscription/purchase required to view.

[78] Google Books Ngram Viewer, use of "joy" between 1800 and 2008 in English corpus, accessed May 5, 2016, https://books.google.com/ngrams/graph?content=joy&case_insensitive=on&year_start=1800 &year_end=2015&corpus=15&smoothing=7&share=&direct_url=t4%3B%2Cjoy%3B%2Cc0 %3B%2Cs0%3B%3Bjoy%3B%2Cc0%3B%3BJoy%3B%2Cc0.

Chapter 11

[79] Daniel J. Levitin, "Why the modern world is bad for your brain," *The Guardian*, January 18, 2015, https://www.theguardian.com/science/2015/jan/18/modern-world-bad-for-brain-daniel-j-levitin-organized-mind-information-overload.

[80] Larry Kim, "Multitasking Is Killing Your Brain," *Inc.*, July 15, 2015, http://www.inc.com/larry-kim/why-multi-tasking-is-killing-your-brain.html.

[81] Zone'in Programs Inc., "Zone'in Fact Sheet: A research review regarding the impact of technology on child development, behavior, and academic performance," Zone'in Workshops, last updated April 26, 2016, http://www.zoneinworkshops.com/zonein-fact-sheet.html.

[82] Dr. Travis Bradberry, "Multitasking Damages Your Brain and Your Career, New Studies Suggest," TalentSmart, accessed May 5, 2016, http://www.talentsmart.com/articles/Multitasking-Damages-Your-Brain-and-Your-Career,-New-Studies-Suggest-2102500909-p-1.html.

[83] Amanda Gardner, "Multitasking Has Its Limits," *Health*, April 15, 2010, http://news.health.com/2010/04/15/multitasking-has-its-limits/.

[84] "Driving Facts," Stop the Texts Stop the Wrecks, last updated September 25, 2015, http://stoptextsstopwrecks.org/tagged/facts?gclid=CKaFjbPw8MsCFdcagQodEsQLcA.

[85] Ian Kerner, "Your smartphone may be powering down your relationship," *CNN*, January 10, 2013, http://www.cnn.com/2013/01/10/health/kerner-social-relationship.

Chapter 12

[86] Nicholas Epley, *Mindwise: How We Misunderstand What Others Think, Believe, Feel, and Want* (New York: Vintage Books, 2014).

Chapter 13

[87] Richard Swenson, *Margin: Restoring Emotional, Physical, Financial, and Time Reserves to Overloaded Lives* (Colorado Springs, Colorado: Navpress, 2004).

[88] Edward Hallowell, *Shine: Using Brain Science to Get the Best from Your People* (Boston: Harvard Business Review Press, 2011).

[89] Kristi Ling, "Is Your Schedule Too Full to Live Fully? 3 Ways to Lighten It Up!" *Kristi Ling* (blog), July 22, 2013, http://kristiling.com/2013/07/22/are-you-taking-on-too-much-3-ways-lighten-your-load/.

[90] Jim Collins, "Good to Great," Jim Collins's website, October 2001, http://www.jimcollins.com/article_topics/articles/good-to-great.html.

Chapter 14

[91] Don Joseph Goewey, "85% of What We Worry About Never Happens," *Don Joseph Goewey* (blog), December 7, 2015, http://donjosephgoewey.com/eighty-five-percent-of-worries-never-happen-2/.

Chapter 15

[92] Martin Merzer, "Survey: 3 in 4 Americans make impulse purchases," CreditCards.com, November 23, 2014, http://www.creditcards.com/credit-card-news/impulse-purchase-survey.php.

[93] Herb Weisbaum, "Guess which gender spends more on impulse," *TODAY News*, November 25, 2014, http://www.today.com/news/guess-which-gender-spends-more-impulse-1D80314130.

[94] Patti Tokar Canton, "Impulsive Spending - or How Not to Spend Money," The Fat Dollar, accessed May 5, 2016, http://www.thefatdollar.com/impulsivespending.html.

[95] Ian Zimmerman, "What Motivates Impulse Buying?" *Psychology Today*, July 18, 2012, https://www.psychologytoday.com/blog/sold/201207/what-motivates-impulse-buying.

[96] Zimmerman, "What Motivates Impulse Buying?" https://www.psychologytoday.com/blog/sold/201207/what-motivates-impulse-buying.

[97] Zimmerman, "What Motivates Impulse Buying?" https://www.psychologytoday.com/blog/sold/201207/what-motivates-impulse-buying.

Chapter 16

[98] Dr. Mark Hyman, "Why Eating Quick, Cheap Food Is Actually More Expensive," Dr. Hyman's website, last updated April 3, 2013, http://drhyman.com/blog/2010/08/13/why-eating-quick-cheap-food-is-actually-more-expensive/.

[99] Hyman, "Why Eating Quick, Cheap Food Is Actually More Expensive," http://drhyman.com/blog/2010/08/13/why-eating-quick-cheap-food-is-actually-more-expensive/.

[100] Crystal Collins, "5 Ways to Make Healthy Eating More Cost-Effective," Clark Howard, February 28, 2014, http://www.clarkhoward.com/5-ways-make-healthy-eating-more-cost-effective.

Chapter 17

[101] "Stress in America Findings," American Psychological Association, released November 9, 2010, https://www.apa.org/news/press/releases/stress/2010/national-report.pdf.

[102] Jennifer Soong, "The Debt-Stress Connection," *WebMD*, reviewed August 12, 2008, http://www.webmd.com/balance/features/the-debt-stress-connection.

[103] Sara R. Collins et al., "Insuring the Future: Current Trends in Health Coverage and the Effects of Implementing the Affordable Care Act," The Commonwealth Fund, April 2013, http://www.commonwealthfund.org/~/media/files/publications/fund-report/2013/apr/1681_collins_insuring_future_biennial_survey_2012_final.pdf.

Chapter 18

[104] Knowledge@Wharton, "Havoc in the Workplace: Coping with 'Hurricane Employees,'" The Wharton School, University of Pennsylvania, November 18, 2013, http://knowledge.wharton.upenn.edu/article/corporate-disaster-zones-coping-hurricane-employees/.

[105] Lauren Montini, "Study: The Extreme Cost of Hiring a Toxic Employee," *Inc.*, April 1, 2015, http://www.inc.com/laura-montini/the-extreme-cost-of-hiring-a-toxic-employee.html.

[106] Travis Bradberry, "12 Ways Successful People Handle Toxic People," *Entrepreneur*, March 17, 2015, http://www.entrepreneur.com/article/243913.

Chapter 19

[107] Thomas Jefferson to John Adams, 21 January 1812, in "The Letters of Thomas Jefferson 1743–1826," American History: From Revolution to Reconstruction and Beyond, http://www.let.rug.nl/usa/presidents/thomas-jefferson/letters-of-thomas-jefferson/jefl213.php.

[108] Margaret Shepherd, *The Art of the Handwritten Note* (New York: Broadway Books, 2002).

[109] *Live Science* staff, "Personality Set for Life by 1st Grade, Study Suggests," Human Nature, *Live Science*, August 6, 2010, http://www.livescience.com/8432-personality-set-life-1st-grade-study-suggests.html.

[110] Sarah Rose Cavanagh, "Your Brain on Friendship," *Psychology Today*, May 30, 2013, https://www.psychologytoday.com/blog/once-more-feeling/201305/your-brain-friendship.

Chapter 20

[111] Holly VanScoy, "Shame: The Quintessential Emotion," *PsychCentral*, October 30, 2015, http://psychcentral.com/lib/shame-the-quintessential-emotion/.

[112] Marilyn Sorensen, *Breaking the Chain of Low Self-Esteem* (n.p.: Wolf, 2006).

[113] Martin E. Seligman, *Authentic Happiness: Using the New Positive Psychology to Realize Your Potential for Lasting Fulfillment* (New York: Atria Books, 2004).

[114] John M. Grohol, "6 Tips to Improve Your Self-Esteem," *PsychCentral*, October 30, 2011, http://psychcentral.com/blog/archives/2011/10/30/6-tips-to-improve-your-self-esteem/.

[115] Marcus Buckingham and Donald Clifton, *Now, Discover Your Strengths* (Washington, DC: Gallup Press, 2013).

[116] Amy Cuddy, *Presence: Bringing Your Boldest Self to Your Biggest Challenges* (New York: Little, Brown and Company) 2015).

[117] Amy Cuddy, "Your Body Language Shapes Who You Are," TED Talks video, 21:02, presented at official TEDGlobal 2012 conference, filmed June 2012, http://www.ted.com/talks/amy_cuddy_your_body_language_shapes_who_you_are.

[118] Edward Hallowell, *Shine: Using Brain Science to Get the Best from Your People* (Boston: Harvard Business Review Press, 2011).

[119] Adam Grant, *Originals: How Non-Conformists Move the World* (New York: Viking, 2016).

Chapter 21

[120] Daniel Pink, *Drive: The Surprising Truth About What Motivates Us* (New York: Riverhead Books, 2009).

[121] Malcolm Gladwell, *Outliers: The Story of Success* (New York: Little, Brown and Company, 2008).

[122] Drake Baer, "Malcolm Gladwell Explains What Everyone Gets Wrong About His Famous '10,000 Hour Rule,'" *Business Insider*, June 2, 2014, http://www.businessinsider.com/malcolm-gladwell-explains-the-10000-hour-rule-2014-6.

[123] Baer, "Malcolm Gladwell Explains What Everyone Gets Wrong About His Famous '10,000 Hour Rule,'" http://www.businessinsider.com/malcolm-gladwell-explains-the-10000-hour-rule-2014-6.

[124] Adam Grant, *Originals: How Non-Conformists Move the World* (New York: Viking, 2016).

[125] Adam Grant, *Give and Take: How Helping Others Drives Our Success* (New York: Penguin, 2014).

Index